CHILDREN ON DEATH ROW
The Hate and the War

By Tommy Lustig

The Lustig Family, at Pilsen, September 1937
Irene, Paul, Tommy

CHILDREN ON DEATH ROW
The Hate and the War

Memories of Surviving the Holocaust and the Iron Curtain

Tenth Edition

By Tommy O. Lustig

Schwanenbruckel Press
Seattle, Washington

Children on Death Row
Copyright 2011
Thomas O. Lenda
All Rights Reserved

Tenth Edition, 1 September 2017

Printed and bound in the United States of America

15 13 12 11 10

ISBN-13: 978-1482782479
ISBN-10: 1482782472

Cover Picture:
The Jewish Cemetery and Crematorium at Terezin.
Phoyto by Tommy Lustig, 2005

Schwanenbruckel Press
Seattle, Washington
www.terezinchildren.com

Se Vzpominkou

na moje rodice Irenu a Pavla Lendu,
a take na deti, ktere prosly Terezinem a nevratily se …

In Memory of

my parents Irena and Paul Lenda,
and the children who passed through Terezin
and did not return ...

I Wish to Thank

My Wife, Rose Lenda and our Daughters, Hana Kern and Helen Lenda, who traveled with me around the world in our escape to freedom, and whose love and assistance inspired this book, and helped me complete it. And also Will Melnyk, who helped to edit this new edition.

Thomas O. Lenda
(Tommy Lustig)
September 1, 2017

Aerial View of Terezin in 2012

Contents

Preface

The Little Boy on Death Row

We, the Jewish Children, were sentenced to death. We just did not know it. We were prisoners, living in the Terezin concentration camp, a holding tank. The prisoners there were gradually transported to a termination camp "in the East," to be murdered – men, women, and children – upon arrival.

Seventy-three years later, I still have a "Forever Dream." I am in a Terezin children's home on a dark, rainy night, in the fall of 1944. I wake up early in the morning, before sunrise. There are some twenty double bunk-beds in a huge barracks room. There is some commotion on the lower level. I see a little group of children in the shadows. They are just getting ready to leave. They are trying not to wake the others.

"Hey Kids, where are you going? Wait for me, Wait for me!"

"We are leaving on a transport to the East. We are leaving to the place of No Return. You will never see us again. You stay back and remember us. And you tell all the people about us. No matter if they like us or not."
"Yes, I will. I promise."

They almost made it. We did not know it then, but they were among the last of the transports to Auschwitz. The rest of us were scared. *Who is going to be next? Why us? What did we do? Who did this to us? Was it the German leader, Adolph Hitler, by himself, or all the German people who started the war, or all who hated us?*

It is a common habit that all people, and all species, dislike other people or other species. If the dislike is intense or notorious, it is called hate. Hate is a very dangerous habit. Hate very often results in a fight, or even in a war in extreme situations. Some leaders, in an effort to become more popular, activate the hate genes of their supporters. This leads to conflict, murder, and war.

This book is about little Tommy, locked up for three years in a concentration camp prison when he was six years old. He was kept in the prison with many other children like him, and all the children were sentenced to death. They were all supposed to be murdered. But some were luckier than others. The murderers ran out of time, and little Tommy survived. This book is not only about the Holocaust, Terezin, and the vanishing children. The story goes beyond the end of World War II, to the Soviet occupation of the Czech Republic.

Tommy, the little boy, that was me. I have changed with time. You will change with time as well, I hope for the better. I will tell you in my writing what I remember from those terrible days. It is my own experience. I was three years old when the Nazis invaded my world. I was nine years old when the war ended and I was freed from one concentration camp. Another started soon after, and it lasted much longer. Stalin, another dictator, dropped an iron wall through Europe, and we happened to be on the East side of it. I will tell you the story of that prison, and my escape from it, in another book.

But this story introduces our family and the environment we were living in. The family history goes back to the year 1765, and to a little village called Schwanenbruckel. It was located on the southern border between Germany and Bohemia (the western part of Czechoslovakia.) It was a family gathering place for many years. Our family was made up of very different Jewish people. Some were rich, and some were not so wealthy, but they were certainly resourceful in ideas. We were a close-knit family, hard-working, and friendly people.

The country we were living in when I was born was called Czechoslovakia, a democratic island in a not too democratic Europe. This was before the Second World War. The whole family saw only too well the threat of Nazi Germany to them, and all the Jewish population. Some of them escaped. Most of them vanished forever, swallowed by the Nazi murdering machine. The story begins with our family life in Pilsen, west of Prague. My father escaped to Prague on the day the Nazis invaded, and my mother followed two weeks later. We settled in a wooded area east of Prague where we lived for three years.

The trip to prison follows, to Terezin concentration camp and the children who lived there. And the story does not end with the Terezin liberation. You will see that there was actually never a complete liberation at all. There was a temporary lifting of the cage, only to have the cage come down again, always more and more forcefully, until we escaped from Czechoslovakia and from Europe, settled for a time in Australia, and finally made it to the United States. The story ends back in a free country. I will tell this part of the story in another book, *Escape to Freedom*.

I have written this book as Tommy Lustig, as that was the name of the little boy I was in Terezin. As I mention in the story, after the war our family changed our name to Lenda, and I am Thomas O. Lenda today.

Life In Terezin

If you have not lived in Terezin, it can be hard to imagine the strangeness of the place. There was an odd and usually unseen juxtaposition between the two Terezins; between the Terezin the Nazis claimed was a "ghetto" (they called it Theresienstadt in German) and the Terezin which the Jewish prisoners experienced mostly as a concentration camp.

The Nazis had, as the world now knows, an agenda, which was to exterminate the Jewish race. Terezin was not an extermination camp, but it was definitely a holding camp, a staging area designed to effectively transport Jews to the extermination camps in the East. No Jew was expected to be a permanent resident of Terezin. Officially we were all in line for those transports; all on Death Row. So the Nazis did not take pains to adequately feed, clothe or house the Jews. This resulted in widespread disease in Terezin, as well as starvation, because of shortages of food, medicines, and other necessities.

The Nazis were well aware of the conditions they were creating inside the walls, and did not want to subject themselves to the rampant disease by inserting themselves into the daily life there any more than what was necessary. As a consequence, the Jewish prisoners were allowed to govern themselves as far as daily life was concerned. The Jewish Elders were the governing body of the Jewish population, though only with regard to relatively insignificant issues, as long as they fully obeyed Nazi policies. There was support from Jewish communities around the world, and this contributed to some sense of civilization. This included care packages of food and other necessities, but it was never enough to relieve the shortages.

In addition, the Nazis were cognizant that, especially as the war progressed, the eyes of the world were upon them. They used Terezin as a "model ghetto," their goal being to whitewash their program of systemic, organized extermination. Their intent was to show the world that they had created a bucolic town where Jews could live out the war happily (and separately.) They even sometimes called it Theresienbad, as if it were a health spa. As time went on, the Nazis allowed musical instruments in Terezin, and permitted many cultural events, including lectures, plays, and concerts.

(Although the artists, and many in their audiences, usually ended up on the next transport to the East.)

So there were two Terezins, the model ghetto, and the harsh concentration camp, existing side by side in cruel irony. While some gathered for a concert in the public square, others were dying in dark attics and damp fortification walls. The person who gave a lecture today on European culture might well tomorrow find himself in a cattle car train headed for Auschwitz. You must understand the two Terezins, to understand what it was like. I have not tried to standardize terminology in this book, because Terezin was always referred to in many different ways.

The Current Book

"Children on Death Row" has been previously published in nine editions, each adding a little to the tale of the hate and the war. This volume is the culmination of many years of telling the story. This volume has been reformatted to enlarge the typeface and margins, eliminate a few duplicate paragraphs, and ensure correct chronological order.

The images I used in this book come from two sources:

Most of the old photographs are from the days before we left for Terezin Concentration Camp. We stored those photographs with some of our good neighbors. There are some photographs from the time after the war when we were living under communist rule. All those pictures were organized by my mother, Irene, and brought to me when my parents came to visit the USA.

There are also those photographs which I made when I was visiting the previous Terezin concentration camp in 2005. It was a nice, sunny day, but most of the buildings show lack of maintenance, and deterioration: an inheritance of the years of communist rule.

I inherited several artist's pictures from my mother. She was given those paintings by some of her patients in the hospital, in appreciation for her help and nursing service. Some of those pictures are also shown in this book.

There are not too many pictures surviving from my actual years in Terezin. We did not have a photo-camera in the concentration camp, because we were prisoners. There are some photographs made by the Nazis for propaganda purposes, but they do not portray the real life of the prisoners at all. However, there are many drawings made by prisoners. Most of those prisoners died a long time ago, during the war. Or, if they survived, they have passed away by now. The pictures they created have been preserved by others, and those pictures are in museums all over the world. I found some of those images with the help of friends, the United States Holocaust Memorial Museum in Washington, D.C., and the internet. I usually show them to the children as part of my educational presentations.

One outstanding exception is a photo – Aerial View of Terezin in 2012 – provided by courtesy of Mr. Ing. Ales Hora and Mr Tomas Hora, THC, of Aerial Photography in Karlovy Vary, Czech Republic.

One last note: I talk about my own experiences only when I make my presentation at schools. That is the ethical requirement. However, in my writing I have included the experiences of my family members and friends as told to me. And, I am not supposed to include any jokes in my presentations. The Holocaust by itself is a very sad story. On the other hand, what is a Jewish story without a joke? Humor was a substantial part of our resistance and survival effort. I had to leave some jokes in.

Thomas O. Lenda
(Tommy Lustig,)
2017

Introduction

Just try to imagine. How could it be that a six year old boy could be locked in a prison and sentenced to death? What kind of a crime could a six year old child have done to deserve a sentence of three years of imprisonment, and to be sentenced to die?

Tommy, the little boy, was actually me, and I am now telling you what I remember from those terrible days more than seventy years ago. I just wanted you to have an image of a little boy in front of you when you hear and read my story, instead of seeing the old man who is writing it now. As you know, *Tempora mutantur et nose mutamur in illis.* Times change, and we change with them. I have changed with the passing of years, and you will certainly change also. I hope my story, the story of little Tommy, will affect the way you change.

Tommy was sentenced to die just because of his race – Jewish – and because of hatred towards the Jewish People. There were about fifteen thousand children in Terezin, all on that Death Row with me, all waiting to be murdered, to be fed to the Nazi murdering machine, to the gas chambers. Out of those fifteen thousand children, most only a little older than me, only a few hundred of us survived.

Six million Jews were killed during the war just because of their race. I hope that in the future you will not judge other children or adults by their origin, or by the race of their parents. I hope that you will not hate each other, or other people. Hating could give an opportunity to fanatics who would use it for their own purpose. In their hunger for leadership and power they would not hesitate to initiate a new war. We cannot afford another war! The weapons available today would almost certainly end all life on this planet – including your own – if there was another war.

So my story is a warning; a warning not to hate other people, not to let people be killed just because of their race, or color of their skin ever again.

My story is also a way to remember the six million Jews who died in the war.

I do presentations to high school children about my war experiences frequently now. In my presentations, and in my writing, I am trying to remind younger generations that the Nazis with their perverse racial theories existed. I am trying to demonstrate the terrible consequences of their racial theories, if applied in practice.

I will concentrate on the country where my family and I lived. Before World War I, it was called Bohemia and Moravia, in the Austrian-Hungarian Empire. At the time of my story, 1936 – 1945, it was called Czechoslovakia. Now it is divided into two states: Slovakia and the Czech Republic. Czechoslovakia was an island of democracy in central Europe. All the surrounding countries were ruled by dictators at the time.

The most powerful of our neighbors was Nazi Germany on the northwest. The Nazis called it "The Third Reich," or Third Empire. (The second Reich had been defeated in World War I. The first Reich was supposedly the Holy Roman Empire.) The Nazis claimed the Third Reich would last "for a thousand years," which is a way of saying "forever." Wishful thinking was always popular in Nazi Germany.

Nazi Germany was a very aggressive state. It was ruled by Adolph Hitler, a brutal and reckless dictator. Hitler was an aggressive public speaker, full of hate, a master in activating his listener's hate genes. Hitler convinced the German people that the world should be rid of minorities such as Jews, Gypsies, Black People, Disabled People, Jehovah's Witnesses, and Homosexuals. He convinced the German people that the Slavs, Asians, and other "lesser" races should be enslaved, and that the German People should rule the world, because the Germans were the best race, the Aryans.

Jews were persecuted in Nazi Germany very harshly. The Nazis had a special plan to deal with the Jews: their goal was to murder all of them, to wipe out the entire race. The Nazis called this plan, "The Final Solution of the Jewish Problem" (*die Endlösung der Judenfrage.*)

Accordingly, the Nazis concentrated on the systematic murder of Jews, as well as many others. The systematic murdering of people because of their race of origin was the Nazi-led genocide, one of the largest genocides in a thousand years. The Nazis were very efficient in their murdering effort. They concentrated on murdering children, to prevent the survival of the Jewish race. I was one of the very few lucky ones who survived the Nazis' highly organized, horrifying murdering agenda. To achieve their murdering goal, the Nazis organized a sophisticated murdering system of six phases:

1. Identification (Registration of the Jews)
2. Expulsion from Society (Separating the Jews from the communities they lived in)
3. Confiscation of Property
4. Ghettoization (Concentrating of Jews in concentration camps and ghettos)
5. Deportation (Relocation of Jews to camps in other countries)
6. Extermination (Mass murdering of the Jews)

You can see how the sixth phase would be the "Final Solution."

First, the Nazis collected information about the Jews, including categories of racial status (full Jewish families, or mixed Jewish families.) They separated the Jews socially from the community they were living in by applying harsh restrictions on them. Then they proceeded to confiscate Jewish property. They removed the Jews from communities in which they lived, "cleansing" communities of certain "undesirable" races such as Jews, Gypsies, and any others as needed to make space for their race, the "Aryan superior race."

Unfortunately, these efforts were nothing new in the history of Europe. But the Nazis reached new depths of horror. Also unfortunately, similar genocidal tendencies in this world did not end with the defeat of Nazi Germany.

The Nazis concentrated the European Jews in "Concentration Camps." One of these camps was Terezin (the Germans called it Theresienstadt,) where I lived for those terrible three years. The primary function of Terezin as a concentration camp was to provide for the temporary storage of live bodies, and to provide a steady supply for the Termination (Extinction) Camps. The Extinction Camps were located mostly in Nazi-occupied Poland, and in the occupied part of the Soviet Union. These camps were equipped with mass gas chambers, masked as shower rooms. The prisoners were taken to the showers right as they arrived at the camp railway station and were selected for extinction (murder.) Only a small portion of the arrivals were selected to stay alive, and work in the camps and nearby factories to support the Nazi war effort.

Even after more than seventy years, the names of these camps still chill the blood:

Auschwitz-Birkenau, Belzec, Chelmno, Majdanek Sobibor, Treblinka.

The fate of the Terezin prisoners in the East was not fully known inside Terezin. But a clue was the fact that nobody returned from "Transports to the East." A substantial part of the horror in Terezin was the waiting for death, to be always on the Death Row.

Towards the end of the war, the Nazis tried to create the impression that Terezin was actually a retirement and recreational facility for the Jews. To do so, the Nazis cleared Terezin of its overcrowded population. They simply loaded tens of thousands of people into cattle trains and transported them to the extermination camps in the East.

As the population in Terezin was reduced, the Nazis went about an extensive ghetto beautification effort. They even went so far as to have a film made, titled "Hitler Gave a Town to the Jews." It showed what a nice life the Jews living in Terezin had, meant to contrast with the horrors most of the European population endured during the war. Not mentioning, of course, that the war was the Nazis' own creation. And this did not change the fact that the Nazis' main effort was to process the people concentrated in Terezin to other places in the East to complete their true goal, to murder them. Terezin was in fact only one of their many murdering system facilities.

I want to show you what the living conditions were in the Terezin concentration camp, specifically for the children. I want to show you what the everyday life of those children was, as I remember it myself. It will help to understand the tragedy of the Nazi murdering effort if

I give you some actual numbers from the Nazis' horrible work results.

The Nazis calculated that there were a total of eleven million Jews living in Europe at the beginning of World War II. This was in Germany, in those countries they directly occupied, in countries that were already under their control, and in countries they expected to take control of when their conquest would be complete.

Before they were defeated, the Nazis managed to murder six million European Jews. And many millions of German people were killed as a result of their war. Many, many millions of people in the countries the Nazis attacked, millions of soldiers and civilians, lost their lives as a result of the war the Nazi fanatics started

Nazi Germany occupied Czechoslovakia partly in 1938 (the Sudetenland,) and fully on 15 March 1939. There were 118,000 Jews living in this country, including my family, and many relatives.

Some 26,000 Jews managed to flee. Most of them had to do a lot of traveling, wandering from one country to another before they were allowed to settle safely and permanently somewhere, spread all over the world. (Some European Jews were denied entry anywhere, and were returned to Europe where they were eventually killed.) The 92,000 Czech Jews who did not manage to flee were relocated to various concentration camps, but mostly to Terezin.

Terezin was a concentration camp not only for Jews from the Czech Republic (at that time the Nazis called it the Protectorate of Bohemia and Moravia) but also from all over Nazi-occupied Europe. The total number of Jewish prisoners who passed through Terezin was almost 140,000.

33,400 prisoners died in Terezin as a result of terrible living conditions – nearly one-fourth of all those imprisoned just because of their race. And 87,000 prisoners were transported to the East, to the termination camps. Out of that number, 3,100 Jews survived – 3.6%.

At the end of the war, 16,800 prisoners were alive in Terezin, almost all of them Jews. Some 1,600 were released to Switzerland and Sweden. Not very many escaped. Several hundred were taken away by the Gestapo, the brutal Nazi secret police.

The Nazis liked to call the Terezin concentration camp a ghetto. However, a ghetto it was not. Ghettos in the past had their own management, usually a council of Elders. There was free business activity, free social activity, and free industrial activity. None of that was present in Terezin. True, there was a council of Elders, but they had to do what the Nazi management ordered them to do. If they did not, or were suspected of not carrying out Nazi orders, they were simply added to the next transport to the extermination camps in the East. Some of the elders were executed in the nearby Small Fortress, the Nazi police prison in Terezin, with a full set of Nazi torture devices. Though the Nazis authorized the printing of special Terezin money, that money was worthless. Nobody could buy anything with it.

The living conditions in Terezin resulted in an unusually high death rate. Terezin was terribly overcrowded. It was an old city fortress, built in 1782 to accommodate approximately 5,000 people, mostly military. There were almost 60,000 prisoners there when our family arrived. The overcrowding created sanitary problems, and of course mental problems for the prisoners as well. Families did not live together. There were old people too sick to function without help. There were children of all ages, and no regular education was permitted. There was insufficient food. Hunger was a permanent condition.

As far as Jewish children were concerned, meaning persons younger than 18 years, there were 18,000 of them in the Czech Republic territory at the beginning of the war. Most of them, about 15,000, went to Terezin; the Terezin concentration camp was their place in the Death Row waiting line. Almost all of those children were gradually transported to the "East," to Auschwitz-Birkenau. They were murdered there in gas chambers upon arrival. Only a few hundred Czech Jewish children survived in Terezin at the end of the war. In my age group of 9 years and younger, there were 48 of us left.

A Note from Tommy

Dear Reader,

You may have noticed me crying when I am talking about my experience in Terezin concentration camp as a six to nine years old prisoner. This is not to catch your attention. The emotional trials of the remembrance of frequent loss of loved ones, close family members and close friends dying or vanishing in transports to unknown places of no return, had a permanent mental effect upon all of us. You probably have noticed also that almost all of the survivors cry, aloud or silently, when they talk about their own experiences or the experiences of others. It happens to us, we cry. Emotional we all are. . . Finally, it appears that it has been noticed by many others as well.

With Love,
Tommy

Terezin Declaration (Excerpt)
Prague Conference, 20 June 2009

Upon the invitation of the Prime Minister of the Czech Republic, we the representatives of the 46 states listed below met this day, 30 June 2009, in Terezin, where thousands of European Jews and other victims of Nazi persecution died or were sent to death camps during World War II.

Recognizing that Holocaust (Shoah) survivors and other victims of Nazi persecution, including those who experienced the Holocaust (Shoah) as small and helpless children, suffered unprecedented physical and emotional trauma during their ordeal. Mindful that scientific studies document that these experiences frequently result in heightened damage to health, particularly in old age, we place great priority in dealing with their social welfare needs in their lifetimes. It is unacceptable that those who suffered so greatly during the earlier part of their lives should live under impoverished circumstances at the end.

1. Albania	2. Argentina	3. Australia
4. Austria	5. Belarus	6. Belgium
7. Bosnia and Herzegovina	8. Brazil	9. Bulgaria
10. Canada	11. Croatia	12. Cyprus
13. Czech Republic	14. Denmark	15. Estonia
16. Finland	17. France	18. FYROM
19. Germany	20. Greece	21. Hungary
22. Ireland	23. Israel	24. Italy
25. Latvia	26. Lithuania	27. Luxembourg

28. Malta   29. Moldova   30. Montenegro
31. The Netherlands   32. Norway   33. Poland
34. Portugal   35. Romania   36. Russia
37. Slovakia   38. Slovenia   39. Spain
40. Sweden   41. Switzerland   42. Turkey
43. Ukraine   44. United Kingdom   45. United States
46. Uruguay

The Holy See *(observer)* Serbia *(observer)*

~~~

Chapter One
We Were Living Peacefully

Me and My Family

I was born on 25 May 1936, the year the Nazis remilitarized the Rhineland and began their march across Europe. We were living in Pilsen, a fairly large and industrial city in a central European country that was called Czechoslovakia at the time. Pilsen is about 60 miles southwest of Prague, the capital of the modern Czech Republic. The city was, and still is, well known for its beer – Pilsner Urquell. Anyone who knows anything about beer knows that Pilsner Urquell is one of the best beers in the world. When I grew into an adult, I drank my share of it, just like almost everyone else in the country. The word *Lustig* in Czech means *Cheerful*, and that was me, Tommy Lustig. Life was still cheerful then, in Pilsen, though dark clouds were beginning to gather.

Pilsen also had a large gun factory named Skoda. It was one of the major heavy weapons suppliers for the Austrian-Hungarian Empire during the First World War. It remained an important weapons manufacturer even after the dissolution of the Empire and the establishment of Czechoslovakia at the end of the war in 1918. The city would soon be desired more for its guns than its beer.

My father, Pavel Lustig, was born in 1904 in the little town of Domažlice, west of Pilsen near the German border. Back then it was part of the western Sudetenland, and was usually known by its German name, Taus. Most of the people who lived there spoke German. My father began attending Czech schools in Pilsen after the family moved there, along with his two younger brothers, my Uncles, Fred and Otto. As they learned Czech, they remained fluent in German also, for their mother, Mina, spoke German only.

As an adult, one of my father's hobbies was officiating at soccer games. He would travel with the local Pilsen soccer team to their games, and officiate there. The locals in the villages were often not happy with his officiating, and he had to run for cover to the next village as fast as he could.

His judgment was very much respected, however, as the eldest cousin of the Klauber family. He would often be sent on investigative missions to find suitable marriage candidates for his younger female cousins. Of course that did not always increase his popularity with those young cousins. Years later, his favorite cousin Rosel would speak of it, and point out how wrong he was not to recommend her beloved Joseph. Well, she married Joseph anyway, and they had a very happy marriage.

In the 1920's my father spent some time in Munich at the Klauber family business. There he got his practical training in the textile business. He traveled as a business representative to the Scandinavian countries and to England. He also studied at a textile industrial college in Manchester, and became fluent in English.

My father was an enthusiastic skier and dancer, and he became a skillful violinist. He played with the Pilsen volunteer symphony orchestra, and quite often also at home, to the delight of his listeners. His younger brother, Fred, was a physician, and his youngest brother Otto, was just completing his studies at the university in Prague to become an attorney.

My Mother, Irena Spitz, was born in Weitra in northern Austria in 1909. Weitra is a small town close to the southern border of Bohemia. The Spitz family moved to the town of Děčin, north of Prague on the Elbe River. She could remember when the river had been swimmable, and she used to swim there as a teenager. She and her two brothers, Leo and Pavu, attend German schools there, so they were fluent in German as well as Czech. She graduated from a local business school as an accountant. Later she also became a certified nurse, and worked in a hospital in Mladá Boleslav before she married my father.

A Note About "Assimilation"

Our family was well assimilated into the Czech community, we thought. We proudly considered ourselves to be Czechoslovakian citizens, of Jewish origin. In reality, however, assimilation into the Czech community was to some extent wishful thinking on the part of the Jews. The Czechs were not so sure about it. This became especially apparent as the threat of a Nazi Germany invasion grew imminent. At that time everyone who spoke German as his first language was suspected of being of German nationality. German nationals were considered to be Nazis, and Nazis were Public Enemy No. 1. Most of the Jews spoke the German language fluently, sometimes even better than Czech, which did not make them popular. In addition, many Jews were part of an intense business competition, not only with the Czechs, but also within the Jewish Community. Naturally, some animosity would surface in such a stressful social environment.

This is a story I was told, which reflects the reality of assimilation in those days:

Mr. Roubicek was the responsible Jewish owner of a family grocery store on the main street in Pilsen. He was a polite and friendly person, especially to all his customers. Sometimes he would stand in front of his store and greet people walking along the street. Most of the people walking by would answer his friendly greeting. Some would venture into the store, where his wife would serve the visitors with politeness.

Once, however, there was a strange newcomer walking along the sidewalk, and he responded harshly:

"Don't greet me, I don't know you!"

Mr. Roubicek tactfully apologized, and invited the stranger into his store. This did not improve the situation, though, and this gruff stranger became a part of the local history.

Mr. Roubicek had many regular customers. Some were Jewish, but most were not. One of them was Mrs. Novak, and her little daughter. Mr. or Mrs. Roubicek would always give the daughter some sweets as a gift, in support of their friendly relationship.

Then, after several years of this friendly relationship, Mr. Roubicek noticed the Novak family had stopped visiting his store. He was still greeting people who walked by on the street, and one day he saw the young Novak girl walking along with her school backpack. So Mr. Roubicek greeted her:

"Good morning, Miss Novak. How are you? I see you are going to school now. How do you like it?"

She answered politely that she liked school very much. Then Mr. Roubicek said he noticed her family was not visiting and shopping in his store anymore.

"Is there anything wrong?" he asked. And the girl answered:

"Well, I was told at school that you Jews have killed our Baby Jesus and we should not visit your store, and we should not buy from you."

Mr. Roubicek answered that he was really surprised to hear this, and said:

"I have never ever killed anybody in my life. I am sure my wife did not kill anybody either. I can assure you of that!"

The little Novak girl insisted that it must be true. She was told this at her school, and the teachers there do not lie. So Mr. Roubicek thought a little, and then offered a solution.

"I am pretty sure it was not me and not my wife. But if you insist, it could have been somebody else. Why don't we go to the police and ask them? They would certainly know about it. They know everything. . ."

But they never did. On the other hand, the police did not know "everything" at that time.

We Were a Big Family Then

My father was very much involved in the local Pilsen community. He published occasionally in local newspapers, and his anti-Nazi feelings were not a secret, assimilation or not.

My paternal grandfather, my father's father Bedrich (Fridrich) Lustig used to own a textile factory in Domažlice. All I know is that the factory burned down one day, and the Lustig family moved east to Pilsen. I visited Domažlice only once with my father after World War II. We walked around the town together, and took a picture in front of one of the houses on the main square. That was the house my father remembered, the house where he was born, and where he lived as a little boy. My grandfather Berich Lustig was still alive when I was little.

My paternal grandmother, my father's mother Mina Lustig, passed away before I came along. Grandma Mina was born in Schwanenbruckel. Her maiden name was Klauber. Most of my relatives who survived World War II and are still alive are from this branch of my family.

Schwanenbruckel was a very small village on the border between Czechoslovakia and Germany. It became a favorite summer gathering place for the whole family in those happy days between the two World Wars.

My father had several stories expressing the feelings of the smart city boys back then. His favorite was about one of the elder uncles who would read the old newspapers stored in the outhouse. He would then surprise the family with long bygone news. Another story was about one of the uncles who brought a new wireless radio, returning from a business trip to Munich. The radio had a dynamo they had to keep turning, and it had individual headphone sets. The uncle let the aunt listen to the miracle: fresh news from as far away as Munich. The aunt commented that this was a nice boy's toy, although even she understood the wireless radio transmission principles quite well. However, she wanted to know how the people in Munich knew that they were supposed to send the news directly to Schwanenbruckel right now! It resulted in a special mission for the uncle: he would have to find out the answer in Munich the next time he went there.

Actually, the smart city boys and girls from Pilsen and Karlovy Vary (Charles-Bath) loved their Schwanenbruckel visits very much. My father would take us there as long as he could, and whenever he could.

Schwanenbruckel as a village did not survive. Several years ago some family members traveled to the place where Schwanenbruckel used to be. They found only a small sign with the village name, and a piece of barbed wire, a typical remnant of the communist government times.

The family tree on the Klauber branch reaches back to the year 1765, when Jacob Klauber was born. The family saga as told by my father was that the Klaubers established a business in hand embroidered handkerchiefs. They would have the handkerchiefs embroidered in the homes of local people in Schwanenbruckel. Then they would collect the finished handkerchiefs and smuggle them over the border to Germany. The Klaubers established an embroidered handkerchiefs store in Munich, and it prospered very well. Most of the Klaubers moved to Munich before World War II. Luckily, they moved to the United States before the war started.

My grandmother's youngest sister, Frieda Klauber, married Heinrich Getreuer and they stayed in Schwanenbruckel. They owned a local general store, and they handled the local embroidery business on the production side. The Klaubers handled the distribution side in Munich.

Schwanenbruckel became a prosperous area thanks to the Getreuers and the Klaubers and their handkerchief business. And this was appreciated by the local people as well. This was until the Nazis took over. The Getreuers moved to Prague. Frieda and Heinrich vanished in the concentration camps of the Holocaust, finally murdered by the Nazis in the gas chambers of Auschwitz. Their children survived, though, escaping to America or China.

My maternal grandfather, my mother's father Otto Spitz, was a supervisor on a farm in Wietra when my mother was born. Wietra is a village on the Austrian side of the border with Moravia, the eastern part of the Czech Republic. The original home of the Spitz family was in a little Jewish community in Novy Etynek, a village in southern Bohemia. All of these places were part of the Austrian-Hungarian Empire at that time, before World War I.

However, the Spitz family became citizens of the new Czechoslovakia when the war ended in 1918. They moved from Austrian Wietra to Czech Děčin, a town in northern Bohemia on the Elbe River. My Grandpa Spitz started a moving company there. He had several horses and wagons, and prospered well. However, he passed away before I came along.

My maternal grandmother, my mother's mother Olga Spitz, was still alive when I was little. Grandma Olga's maiden name was Popper.

My grandfather Otto Spitz's parents were born in Novy Etynek, and they had nine children.

Almost all the family members from my mother's side vanished during the Holocaust.

Chapter Two
The Nazi Takeover

Nazi Germany's intention to occupy Czechoslovakia was no secret. The Nazis wanted to exploit the highly developed industry and skillful workforce of the country. Specifically, facilities like the Skoda gun factory were of interest to their expansion plans. Nazi Germany strongly supported local Nazi sympathizers and their organizations, to prepare the environment for their invasion.

Nazi Germany took over the northern, western and southern border regions of Czechoslovakia, the Sudetenland, in October of 1938 as a result of the Munich Treaty between Great Britain, France, Italy, and Germany. The border area was the area where mostly German people lived, and also where most of the Czechoslovak border fortifications were. Schwanenbruckel and Karlovy Vary (Charles-Bath) where our relatives lived were in the Sudetenland also. (Schwanenbruckel later became part of the border "no-man's-land" when the Communist government took over after the war, and the iron curtain fell down right there.) The Munich Treaty was considered to be a treaty of betrayal by many. Before the treaty's approval, Great Britain and France had a mutual defense agreement with Czechoslovakia in case of an aggressive invasion. But the simple fact was that Great Britain and France were not prepared for a war. They were not strong enough at that time to resist a war-prepared Nazi Germany. In addition, Germany also had a non-aggression agreement with the Soviet Union in preparation. That agreement was supposed to be secret, but it was well-known to the British and French governments, as we know now.

It turned out the Munich betrayal treaty was right in line with a pragmatic rule: Don't start a fight if you know you cannot win. The Munich Treaty was considered to be a peace-saver by some people in France and Great Britain. In fact, it encouraged Nazi Germany to proceed with its aggressive plans.

A few months later, on 9 November 1938, the Nazis organized a general attack on Jews and their property all over Europe, wherever they could find some sympathizers. It was called *Kristallnacht* (Crystal Night, or Night of Broken Glass.) The Nazi sympathizers concentrated their destructive effort on breaking Jewish glass items such as shop windows, but also on Jewish religious items such as synagogues and cemeteries. Some Jews were physically attacked, too, and some were imprisoned or sent to the first concentration camps, such as Dachau. The whole event was generated personally by Adolph Hitler, the Nazi leader. It was meant to avenge the assassination of a German embassy employee in Paris by a young Jew (which had been, in turn, revenge for Nazis forcefully running some German Jews out of Germany into Poland – including the young Jew's parents.)

It was probably around that time – between the Nazi takeover of the fortified Czech border area without a fight and the full time occupation of Czechslovakia and the division of the country into two parts (the Protectorate of Bohemia and Moravia, and Slovakia) that some Nazi sympathizers used explosives to blow up the Jewish Cemetery in Pilsen. But there was an accident: in blowing up the cemetery the Nazi agents blew themselves up also.

The Pilsen Jewish community, of which my family was a part, was upset by the destruction of their cemetery. But at the same time they saw it as moral encouragement. They would say, "God is on our side, and nothing can happen to us." This is not exactly what the Lustig family would say. Our motto was that God helps those who help themselves.

The complete Nazi invasion of Czechoslovakia became a reality on 15 March 1939. I was almost three years old when Nazi Germany occupied Pilsen on that date. My father, whose anti-Nazi sentiments were well known, escaped the same day to the east, to Prague. It was a very difficult action, because the main road from Pilsen to Prague was fully occupied by the Nazi army in their effort to take over the capital city as soon as possible. So my father had to use all possible side roads to reach Prague without confrontation with the new governing authority. He told me later that he was scared of the Nazis, and rightly so.

My mother was invited to the newly established office of the Gestapo in Pilsen several days after the invasion. The Nazi brutality against Jews was already well known by that time. Stories of the Nazi treatment of people they disliked, not only Jewish people, preceded the Nazis all over Europe. My mom took me with her to the police station. She expected the Gestapo would have to send her home after all, because they would not be comfortable keeping a little child there. She was questioned about my father's whereabouts, but she knew nothing, and we were sent home again. After that, she organized the family's move to the Prague suburb of Radesovice, where my father found a small house for rent. My mom and I were out of Pilsen within two weeks of the Nazi occupation.

(My mom used the same tactic again some ten years later, when Stalin was in power in Russia. She was "invited to visit" a Communist police office in a nearby regional town. That time she took my brother, who was ten years younger than me. She was questioned about her "frequent" correspondence with people in the West, the countries outside the territory ruled by the Communist regime, outside the Iron Curtain. The correspondence was with some friends and family members who had survived the Nazi Holocaust, and the police knew it. They had opened almost all of her letters, and closed them up again. But it seems that was a time consuming and expensive chore, so they wanted to scare her out of her communication habit. She was told that she was suspected of providing some information to the enemies in the West, and therefore she should stop it, or at least minimize her correspondence, or else. . . However, she and my brother made it safely home again.)

Life in Radesovice

We settled in Radesovice, some twenty miles east of Prague. The relocation turned out to be a very smart move. My father would have been imprisoned by the Pilsen Gestapo right at the beginning of the occupation, and most likely he would not have survived. The relocation also postponed our family deportation to the Terezin concentration camp by almost a year. That also gave us a better chance to survive. The Jews from Pilsen were among the first to be sent to Terezin, to make Pilsen a Jew-free city (on 18, 20, and 22 January 1942.) Most of the Pilsen Jews did not survive the Holocaust.

I hardly comprehended what was happening when the Nazis took over the country we lived in. I was just three years old. Some memories come back to me when I look at old photos. Other memories were generated when my parents talked about some of the events where I had been present, or where I was the center of the action.

My only memory from the first days in Radesovice is our trip to Prague in our small Tatra automobile. We went to visit my Grandfather Lustig and my father's brothers. My parents asked me what I would like to see during this trip. It would be our last visit to Prague, because the automobile had to be made unusable. The car had to be set up on wooden blocks and stripped of its wheels. These had to be given to the Nazis, because the Nazi army was short of rubber and other materials needed for their military vehicles. Nazi Germany did not have access to many natural resources, so a material recycling effort was strictly enforced.

I remember it was a nice day. We drove all over the beautiful city of Prague to see the historical buildings, views of the river Vltava, the historic bridges, and the castle. A Nazi flag was flying at the castle instead of the Czechoslovak President's flag as it used to be. My parents wanted to see all the places they remembered, the places to which their memories were attached. I just liked to look at the river from the top of the hills.

It was the last time I saw the car. My father parked it in a rented garage not too close to the house we lived in. Our own travel became very limited from then on. Our friends and family members would have to come to visit us, and they did. I was now the only one in the family who had a moving automobile! At first, it was "Tommy's Mercedes." But one day a visiting Jewish friend pointed out to us that I was probably the only Jew who was driving a Mercedes now. Mercedes was the automobile Adolph Hitler used, and therefore it was a no-no for Jews to own and drive one. So I changed the name of my automobile from Mercedes to Tatra, as my father's Tatra was no longer in use and there would be no problem of confusion and mix-up anymore.

My father told our relatives and friends that we could not travel around anymore, and that they were welcome to visit us. It was actually my father's habit to invite anybody he met. He would explain how to get to our place by train, by autobus, or by car. The last part from the main road to our home was a bit tricky. He would tell them that we might not be at home when they would show up, as we did not have a telephone to call first, and cell phones had not been invented yet. So he would say that they could open the little door in the fence by simply kicking it with their left foot, and feel free to come inside. We would certainly show up shortly. If they asked why they should use their left foot and not their hand, he explained that their hands would be busy holding all the gifts they would be bringing!

Indeed, most of the visitors would actually bring some toys for me, and I got spoiled. I would ask them right when they came, "Uncle, what did you bring me?" This was embarrassing to my parents and they told me that I should not do this. So I changed my tactic, and I would ask, "Uncle, what do you have in your briefcase?" It was somewhat better, but still not acceptable!

My parents were very concerned about my health, and wanted me to be ready for the rough conditions in the concentration camp the Nazis prepared for us. They arranged with the local physician to treat me with a tanning lamp on a regular basis. It used tubes filled with mercury. Then I heard one day from a visitor that the hot mercury could break out of the tube and spill on the patient lying on the bed under the lamp. I became scared, and from that moment, whenever the timer would ring, I would jump up and run away to the waiting room as fast as I could! So my parents started to search for the visitor who had left the bad rumor for me, so that he could come back and deny his story. Finally, the tanning treatment was terminated after several of my embarrassing running exercises, and I was at peace again.

The Nazis started to oppress Czech Jews the same way they did in Germany. New oppressive regulations were issued very frequently. There were restrictions on what jobs Jews could have, whether they could sell property, or go to school, when and where they could shop, use busses and trams, where they could travel, and many other things.

We lived in Radesovice for three years. My father was not allowed to continue to work as a business representative of a textile manufacturer. He was only allowed to do manual labor. He found a job in a nearby chemical factory and he traveled there every morning. However, he was fired after a short time when some co-workers complained that they did not want to work with a Jew. After that, he found another manual job at a sawmill, not too far from where we were living. Sometimes my mother and I visited my father at the sawmill, to bring him lunch. He was not used to such manual work, and his eyesight was not too good, either. Then he had an accident where he cut his hand, and he was out of work for a while again.

Next to the house we lived in was another similar apartment house, also rented by two Jewish families. One of them was the Riesel family. They had two boys just a few years older than me. I often played with them or, more precisely, they played with me. For my fifth birthday I was given a red railway station manager's cap, and a train stop sign. I played the railway station manager, and the other boys were passengers. But they insisted that a good station manager had to endure heavy rain also. To prove this, I had to suffer water being poured on my new red cap! My parents were not too pleased with this, and I remember they let me know it. But most of the time the games with the Riesel boys were bearable. One day the Riesels were gone, and we never heard from them again.

Our other neighbors were the family of my father's friend, Charles Sonnenshein. Except that it was only his wife Wilma, with their little daughter Vera, who was the same age as me. Charles had left for England just before the Nazis came. The family was supposed to follow as soon as he found some accommodation there, and some means of existence. But the Nazis invaded in the meantime, and it became very difficult to leave. So they were waiting for an exit visa, I believe.

Vera and I played hide and seek sometimes. Once when we were in the woods near the apartment houses, where the trees were big and tall, Vera had to go to the bathroom. She peed squatting down as girls do, and I told her that was not the way to do it. I was always full of good advice, called "aicess" (unsolicited advice in Jewish slang.) I told her that there was a more efficient way to pee, and I demonstrated! Vera said that she could not do it that way because she did not have what I had. That was a surprise to me! I asked her if she had had surgery where the physician operated on her and cut it off. She did not remember anything like that. For some reason, we did not play outside together any more after that. . .

One evening, Vera's mom Wilma and my uncle Pavu rode bikes to the neighboring village to buy some meat from a farmer. It was already dark as they were returning home. Suddenly they saw a local policeman on the road. Immediately they threw the package of meat into the woods, but it was too late. The policeman stopped them, picked up the package, and asked to see their documents. Of course he confiscated the meat and concluded that they were Jews traveling in the evening (after curfew) without the mandatory yellow star on their clothes. And they were found in possession of a package of meat that was obviously from black market sources. They were released, but a police report was sent to the Nazis. The result of this accident was that they were sent to the Terezin concentration camp on the next available transport. We never saw Wilma or Vera again. Pavu was still in Terezin when we got there. My grandmother had gone to Terezin even earlier than Pavu. Another of my mother's brothers, Leo, volunteered to go with her. We never saw them again.

But still, we kept doing a lot of the things we were not supposed to do. My uncle kept his bike until the last minute. We were not supposed to exercise or do sports such as our favorite skiing, and we were supposed to give our skiing gear to the Nazi authorities. But we kept skiing in the neighborhood for two more winters after the Nazi takeover.

I was not supposed to be educated; I was not supposed to go to school. Not that I would mind. But my parents got some educational books for me, to learn letters and numbers, and to remember all that. So some knowledge was forced upon me, whether I liked it or not! It seems to me now that we just did not take the Nazis too seriously. But, bit by bit, they kept prevailing. Starting 1

September 1941 all Jews had to wear a yellow star with the letters "*JUDE*" ("JEW" in German) on their clothes. I still remember how my mom and my grandma sewed the yellow stars with some not too polite comments about the Nazis' brain capacity and their return to the thinking and habits of the Middle Ages.

Pearl Harbor was attacked by the Japanese while we were in Radesovice, on 7 December 1941. It was a terrible, unheard-of slaughter of sailors and civilians on a peaceful Hawaiian island. The United States declared war on Japan immediately.

This is a related story I was once told:

It happened some forty years after the attack, around 1981. Three young professional friends, Sam, Kim, and Steve, were sharing an apartment in downtown San Francisco. In general, there was a very friendly atmosphere in the apartment, most of the time.
Sam came home one evening from the local pub. It happened to be on the anniversary of the Pearl Harbor attack. Sam was unusually excited that evening. He went to Kim as directly as he could and hit him quite strongly, out of nothing. Surprised, Kim asked, "What is this for?" to which Sam replied that this was for Pearl Harbor. Kim thought a little, and said that the Pearl Harbor attack was by the Japanese, and it happened some forty years ago. In addition, he himself was not Japanese anyway; he was of Korean origin. To which Sam replied, "Doesn't matter. You Asians are all the

same anyway." And this was the end of it, at least for some time.

Several months later, on 15 April, Kim came home in the evening, went directly to Sam, and hit him not too gently either. Surprised, Sam asked, "What was this for?" to which Kim replied "This was for the Titanic." Sam was thinking intensely, and after a while said, "That was an iceberg," to which Kim explained readily as well, "Iceberg, Greenberg, Rosenberg, doesn't matter. You Jews are all the same anyway."

The third one in the party, Steve, was a newly arrived European immigrant. He was just watching, listening, and wondering, "Is this the America I was dreaming of?"

This was now some thirty years ago. America has changed a lot since then, mostly for the better, but we still have a long way to go. And those friends? They lived happily ever after.

One day, just as we were about to leave for the Terezin concentration camp, my father came home from work and told us how he had outsmarted the Nazis this time. He had gone to the garage and had the central driving axle removed from the car. Then he had dug a hole in the ground in a secret place, and buried the axle there. He explained to us that now the car could not be taken away because this particular axle was unique to that particular car. It was factory fitted, and was irreplaceable. When we came back from the concentration camp we would find our car where he had left it, he said. And that would be soon, anyway. Little did he know how well the Nazi system for collecting Jewish property had really worked.

Finally it came. We had expected it for some time. The printed notice told us to present ourselves with our belongings, not exceeding fifty kilograms per person, at the Exhibition Hall in Prague on the date written in by hand: 12 September 1942. That was it.

~~~

Chapter Three
Transport to Terezin

The Transport

There was not much to pack. There was not much we could take with us, anyway. It would not be more than three weeks or so, our wishful thinking told us. The Third Reich, which was to last a thousand years according to Hitler's promise to the German people, was almost finished, we believed. The Nazis were at war with the entire civilized world at that time already, and they were experiencing substantial losses on the battlefields, according to rumors. We of course disregarded some of the Nazi victories as short-lived accidents. Nobody expected that it would take another three long years before we would see soldiers in different uniforms. In any event, it was incomprehensible that one could leave all of one's possessions behind and just walk away forever. My parents each had one fifty kilogram (110 pounds) suitcase and I had a small army bread pack (or back pack) over my shoulder. It was full of batteries for flashlights. There was a flashlight in the back pack, too, and another flashlight with a little dynamo in it, just in case the three weeks were extended and we ran out of batteries. I was very proud of it: I was also helping out in this unfortunate situation our family was in.

Indeed we made some provision in case the war would drag on past the estimated three weeks. We hid some of our valuable possessions by moving them to some of our good friends for temporary safekeeping. This was done secretly, because these friends risked facing substantial difficulties if discovered.

My parents had to fill out lots of forms and take those forms with them to the assembly place in Prague. They had to provide an inventory of all our property and assets. Everything we owned had to stay in our apartment, except the fifty kilogram suitcases we were taking with us. All our furniture, valuables, savings, automobile, and our apartment house in Pilsen were taken away from us at once. Our property was the result of my parents' hard work, and partly the hard work of their parents, and their grandparents and their great-grandparents. Our property was not our property anymore. It all became the property of Nazi Germany.

On the designated day we went to the local railway station, and went by train to downtown Prague. From there we went to the Exhibition Hall, and reported in at the entrance.

Our transport number was "BG." There must have been about a thousand Jewish people there, probably more. There were people everywhere. I was not used to mingling with so many people at once. There were public toilets and there were public washrooms. There were lines of people waiting for their turn, as everything was always full and in short supply. We had to stand in line for the food, and it was not too good, either. At that time I was still spoiled and quite selective of what I liked to eat and what not. However, this habit did not last for too long.

We were assigned a place with mattresses on the floor in a big exhibition hall, and lay down to sleep in the evening. Suddenly an order was announced in German, "Achtung!" Not too many people knew what to do, but it spread around that everybody, including the able children, had to stand up and listen. So we did. It was supposed to be a military drill, as the Nazis liked to be strict and efficient. We were told some organizational matters, mainly that we would be sent to Terezin by train in three days. We were told that our luggage would be taken care of. We had with us only what we could carry to the railway station anyway. In the morning, we were organized by the numbers we had been given at the entrance. My number was BG 575. I still remember that, because I had to memorize it, and was told not to forget it, ever.

There were several railway stations in Prague, but I believe we went from the Exposition Hall complex to the nearest station, Bubny, just a few blocks away. But it took at least half of the day before everybody was situated on the train, in the place designated for him. Finally, the train started to move. We were all being taken to a prison, and the prevailing majority never made it back again. In fact, this was the last civilized life experience for me for quite a while. For almost three years. But, ironically, we were sort of glad that something was happening. We traveled in an ordinary, old-fashioned train. It was not 1st Class, but a decent 2nd or 3rd Class, not like the transports further to the East, when cattle cars were used.

The countryside passed by, the train went along

the Elbe River, and after a few hours we stopped at the small railway station of Behusovice, from which we had to walk about 3 kilometers to Terezin. Terezin at that time did not have a railway station. The railway line was extended to Terezin later, mainly to transport people to the extermination camps in the East.

Our luggage was taken from the train and loaded onto carts pushed by people already living in Terezin, the Transportation Team or *Transportleitung* Organization. The carts were actually old Jewish funeral carriages with the tops cut off, resulting in flat carts. They were driven and pushed by people instead of horses as originally intended. It turned out luckily that one of the Transportleitung Organization people happened to be my Uncle Pavu, my mom's younger brother. He took special care of our luggage.

We took our hand luggage and walked. I had the small old army bread pack loaded with flashlights and spare batteries. It should have lasted for those three weeks we all believed it would take for the Nazi military machinery to collapse, and we could return home again. It was actually a nice and sunny, pleasant, warm day, even with not such pleasant circumstances for us. But it was still a day to remember forever. There were the Transportleitung Organization people to organize the newly arrived people in five-row columns for the 3 kilometer walk to the prison. I was six years old on that walk to Terezin.

We walked from the railway station on a country road with trees on the sides, and a nice view of the wide countryside, probably the last butterflies to be seen. It was actually quite pretty, for a while. Soon I started to feel the bread pack pressing on my shoulder. I kept on, but moved it from one shoulder to another. There was no help in sight; everybody had to carry his own bag. Although the large 50 kg suitcases were on the carts, our 3 kilometer hike became an exhausting experience for me.

At last, the old brick fortress town walls appeared. Presently, we walked into the Terezin concentration camp, although the Nazis called it Theresienstadt, and called it a ghetto. It became my prison for the next three years of my young life. At that time, nobody thought that it would take such a long time before we would see the fortress from the outside again.

The fortress town was originally built by the ruler of the Austrian-Hungarian Empire, Joseph II, in 1780, and it was named in honor of his mother, Maria Theresa. It was planned for some 5,000 people, including the military personnel. There were almost ten times more Jewish prisoners, some 58,000 of them, crowded into this fortress town when we arrived. And 156 of those Jewish prisoners died on that day in September 1942 due to the harsh living conditions.

For us, it was a shock. There were so many people all around us, everywhere. It was already late in the afternoon and we were quite exhausted. We entered the *Slojska* building. In local slang, "*slojsovat*" meant to steal. That was what was happening in this place. It was something like a terminal customs hall, except that it was located in an old brick building, probably part of the original city fortifications structures. This was supposed to be a check-in station for the ghetto entry. Every piece of luggage was to be put on a desk and opened. Nazi officers and civilians did the inspection with their eyes and hands busy. They took out anything considered unacceptable for the prisoners to possess. I don't remember any arguments or negotiations. The new prisoners were scared and tired.

Of course some prisoners who had some relatives with the Transportleitung Organization had some advantages. So it happened that our belongings bypassed the *Slojska* ("Sluice") process, as my Uncle Pavu was able to move it past the Nazi inspection. We were getting our first training in the way business was done in Terezin. We had to learn much more, and fast.

The First Days

It was late in the evening when we finally ended up in our new accommodations. Remember, at that time I was six years old. I had never been too far from my mother, and my father was close to me most of the time as well. We used to live in a modest, but nice apartment in a villa, right next to a forest, in a small rural village. We had a relatively decent living standard, considering the wartime circumstances. The country had already been under Nazi occupation for three years, and the Jewish population was certainly not a privileged group. On the contrary, they were persecuted more than other Czech citizens. I would have already started school under normal circumstances, but under the Nazi regulation this was out of the question. Jewish children were not supposed to be educated at all.

Our new accommodations were in a large attic. It

was the top floor of an old barracks building, Podmokly Barracks, just under the roof. It was a huge dark space, and we shared it with hundreds of people, mice, and rats. Wooden planks and plywood boards had been placed across the big beams on the attic floor. We were given empty sacks that we had to fill with straw from the yard. Then we dragged them up the stairs and placed them on the plywood boards in our designated place at the attic door, as the rest of the attic was already taken. This was our sleeping space, and also our living space. It was a big, open, dark space to me. It was a tunnel with no light at the end. Except that we had our batteries and flashlights, thanks to me. I was a proud little boy again, at least for a while.

There was a mysterious crowd of other people in the attic all around us, on the right, on the left, and behind us. There was a big steel entry door in front of us, and the staircase down to the lower floor. It was so overwhelming. And it was not a very friendly atmosphere, either. Everybody had to struggle for his living space. It certainly created a very strong motivation to get a permanent work assignment. This was the prerequisite for hopefully better quarters. Nothing could be worse than what we had, we thought. It was understood that this was a temporary arrangement, and we braved it out. We did not have any other choice. For me, it was also an adventure, at least at the beginning.

The most important part of my adventure was how to get to the toilets and washrooms. We had to go down one floor, and there were large common washrooms and toilets accessible from an open corridor. There was no privacy, upstairs or downstairs. Upstairs, where we lived and slept, was a big, open attic: no walls, no partitions. The only "privacy" was the permanent darkness, from time to time illuminated by a flashlight. Downstairs was full of people, young and old, and some children. All people seemed to be concentrated in one big corridor, at the common toilets or common washrooms. This was the standard arrangement in the old three-story barracks, but it was all new to us.

The food was served military style. We had metal military dishes and utensils. Somewhere there were large kitchens where the food was prepared for all the people in the concentration camp, and distributed to various barracks and work sites. We stood in a line, and some food was given or thrown into the dishes. It was hardly edible. At that time I was probably still too spoiled to appreciate the food. But my attitude towards food changed soon, and permanently. There was a very good cook in place: hunger.

"Irena, did you see the two men with the stretcher this morning?"

"Yes, I did. What was it about?"

"They were picking up an old man who died during the night. He was over there, in the corner of the attic, all by himself. They had to chase away a big rat that was nibbling on the dead man's face."

"Maybe we should be a little careful of what we say in front of the children. It will scare them for the rest of their lives."

"You mean your little one? He will learn these realities in life anyway, the sooner the better. The rats

carry fleas, and the fleas carry diseases, so one has to be careful. By the way, one has to be careful about the bed bugs. You have to look under your blanket on the board with a flashlight before you go to bed. You can catch them with a wet bar of soap just by pressing it down on them."

"Well thanks. There is always something new to learn, every day, sometimes every minute."

"Well, every day has plenty of minutes, as long as you are alive. After that, you don't have to worry anymore."

The weather also changed for the worse soon after our arrival. This was in line with my mother's proven belief that the weather is always nice 'til the end of the Jewish New Year holidays, and then it changes. It did also on this year, 5703. The weather became rainy and cold soon after we arrived, and this did not help us in our misery.

I heard my parents talking quietly in the darkness:

"Pavel," my mom said, "we have to get out of this. There has to be some way. This is unbearable."

"Yes we do," my dad answered. "We are supposed to get some work, the sooner the better. There is an office in another building and they will assign us to something. There will be separate accommodations for women and men."

"Maybe we could do something about this. After all, we are a family, so that should at least give us a separate room for the three of us."

"I am afraid we are out of luck on this one, Irena. Separate rooms are at a premium in this over-crowded ghetto. Only some of the prominent families have the privilege of having their own room."

"What prominent privilege, Pavel? Aren't we supposed to be equal in this Jewish ghetto?"

"Well, this is not actually the French Revolution. And since when are people in Jewish ghettos all equal? I don't remember that equality of people was noted in the Torah or in the Talmud. But I would admit that religious education is not my strongest point. Also, this is not actually a Jewish ghetto, as I see it. It is more like a Nazi concentration camp. And I doubt if Hitler has anything about equality in his book "My Struggle" (*Mein Kampf.*) On the other hand, he may have something along the lines of, 'The Jews are all the same. . .'

"As far as Tommy is concerned, they have some kind of Kinderheims for the children. Somewhat similar to a boarding school. Although they ae not supposed to teach them anything."

"This is awful," my mom said. "Tommy should have started school just about now."

"We will see what we can do about it," my dad answered. First things first . . . Well, after all, if others can cope with this, we can too. And, hopefully, it is not for too long, anyway. Although it may take longer than our original estimate of several weeks."

~~~

Chapter Four
Growing Up in Prison

Two Soldiers Lost In the Desert

The first American action related to the European War Theater was the invasion of North Africa on 12 November 1942. It was two months after our family's imprisonment in Terezin concentration camp.

This is a relevant story I was told:

It is about two Jewish soldiers, Joe and Sam, lost on their military mission in the desert. Finally, after several exhausting days of wandering, they ran into two other soldiers. Unfortunately, it was two Nazi SS officers. These SS were not in much better condition, as they were exhausted as well. To survive, they needed what the Jews had, and the Jews needed what the SS had. They agreed that only two of the four could survive.

The Nazi officers declared that they were obligated to survive and kill the Jews. This was because the Germans were of the Aryan race, and their mission and destiny was to kill the Jews, and in doing so they would save life on earth. The Jewish soldiers were completely exhausted, and said that there was nothing they could do about it. Then Joe pointed out that everybody sentenced to death has the right to have his last wish fulfilled.

The SS reluctantly agreed. So Joe said that his last wish was to be given three strong Nazi quality punches to

*his face. The SS agreed, and one of them provided the
last wish, immediately and with pleasure.*

*At that, Joe reached for his pistol and shot the two
SS officers on the spot!*

*The two Jewish soldiers took the Nazi supplies,
including their map and compass, and they started to
walk, not talking at all. They found their unit before
sunset. Suddenly, Sam could not stand it anymore and
asked Joe, the shooter, why he hadn't shot the Nazis right
when they met them.*

*So Joe explained: "I could not shoot the German
soldiers just because they were German and just because
they were themselves victims of Nazi propaganda. I had
to have a reason: I had to get really upset." (But he
actually used another more popular military expression!)*

Our Family is Broken Up

My parents started to look for a more suitable
accommodation alternative quite actively, almost
immediately after our arrival. There was, of course, great
encouragement: the temporary accommodation in the
barracks' attic being overcrowded, with no light except
flashlights, common facilities one floor down, and rats
nibbling on dead people overnight.

Remember, we used to live in Pilsen, and then in
Radesovice, quite comfortably before we went to the
prison, to Terezin. Naturally, as a family, we lived
together in an apartment. We had several rooms in
addition to the kitchen and bathroom. Suddenly it turned
out that we would each have to live separately in this
Terezin ghetto the Nazis had prepared for us. At least we

could see each other almost daily.

In order to obtain a permanent accommodation, a work assignment had to be obtained first. This depended upon education and prior experience, but also upon the right connections. My mom, Irene, was a graduate from a business school, an accountant. However, every second Jew seemed to be an accountant, and there was not too much use for accountants in Terezin anyway. Therefore, this was not the profession she would pursue in Terezin. But she was also a certified nurse, and she had some valuable experience, as she had practiced this profession for several years before she married my father. This was a profession very appreciated in Terezin. There was a large hospital in one of the barracks, and there was also accommodation for the nurses in one wing attached to the main building. It was a crowded accommodation. The bunk beds were stacked three levels high, one above another. But it was certainly much better than the accommodation in the barracks' attic where we lived since we came to Terezin.

Paul, my father, was also a graduate from a business school, and had several years of education at a technical textile college in England. However, there were too many Jews in Terezin who had a textile and accounting background. And, again, there was hardly any use for that in Terezin.

It appeared that Paul did not have any special Terezin-usable qualifications except one: he had some good friends, and of course relatives, and that was what mattered most. This most important qualification was a result of his basic mental gift or approach to life: help your neighbor in need whenever you can. Because of this special qualification, he could join the Transportleitnung corps. He was accommodated with other men from the same department. This accommodation was in a huge but dark room in one of the many barracks. The bunk beds there also were stacked three levels high, and there were plenty of them in that room.

My New Home

Now the problem was what to do with me, six-year-old little Tommy. Terezin had homes for children of all ages, something like a local boarding school. Officially, they could not be associated with the word "school," because the Nazi governors of Terezin strictly forbade the teaching of Jewish children. So these institutions were simply called "home," or "Heim" in German.

Irene, my mom, brought me to the Heim I was assigned to. It must have been soon after our arrival in Terezin, probably not more than a week or two. I was still totally confused. The only thing I understood was that my mom would leave me there with all the strange people, and it did not make me happy at all.

My Heim was a large, one room establishment. It was located in Dresden Barracks, one of the original barracks built by Joseph II some two hundred years ago. Originally, the room was meant to accommodate troops. It was connected with one set of large doors to the common open corridor, where a lot of people were moving back and forth all the time. We saw bunk beds everywhere, once we were inside the room, with the large door closed behind us. There were two windows far ahead on the other side of the room. The bunk beds were the main furniture, and were only two levels high, and a little smaller than the adults' bunk beds. This was an allowance made for children only.

There was a corridor in the middle leading to the other side where the windows were. There was also a common place along the window wall, with a table in the middle. The children's bunk beds were placed along the corridor, and along the walls. Two larger bunk beds were at the windows wall, at one corner. This was for the supervisors. The two larger bunk beds had a blanket hanging down from the upper bed to provide some privacy for the supervising ladies living in one large room with all the young boys living all around them.

Allocation of sleeping space for the young boys was a complex procedure. The youngest boys were usually placed on the bottom beds. Not that they would not know how to get to the upper bunk, there was a ladder available for almost every upper bunk. But there were still some younger boys who would find themselves wet in the morning, and it was not desirable to have the wetness coming down from the upper bunk upon the lower sleepers. For me, this situation was rather rough. I was never before too far from my mother or father. Suddenly I was on my own, and I did not take it well.

There were a lot of boys there, about my age, or maybe older. At that time I did not have any idea about numbers, so "a lot" was my closest estimate. Most likely there were some forty boys and Gerta, our supervisor. We were not supposed to call her "Miss Teacher" as was common in ordinary schools. We called her by her first name, Gerta, as if she was one of us. We did not use the polite form of the word "you" – "*vy*" – as is common in the Czech language when children talk to adults (except family members,) but simply "Gerta" or "you." ("*ty*").

Hana was another supervisor, and we called her Hanka as would be common if she was one of us. Hanka used to live in Prague. She came to Terezin in the same transport as our family did, and she appeared at the Heim at the same time as I did. Sometime later, Gerta got married in a nice wedding ceremony. That was an exception in Terezin, and not an exception appreciated by the Nazis. So the newlyweds went together on a "honeymoon trip" in a transport to the East almost right after the wedding. We never heard of them again.

We got Erna as another supervisor after Gerta vanished in the transport. Another supervisor appeared later. She was an older lady who spoke German only. This had some educational benefit for us: we had a forced opportunity to learn the German language.

Gerta and Hanka were young, probably about twenty years old. Gerta was most likely a teacher by profession. I know for sure Hanka was a teacher. Both of them were very practical young ladies, as the circumstances required. They had to deal not only with the children but also, more daringly, with the parents who were new and not used to such an arrangement. The parents expected much more than could be provided, and it took a while before the new arrivals realized that everyone was trying to do their best under the given circumstances. Hanka told me many years later that she still remembered how angry my mom was with her because my socks kept disappearing.

Bullying

Gerta's welcoming introductory speech to me was polite in form, but very rough in substance as far as I was concerned. In addition to explaining the routines and rules of engagement, some practical warnings were added. Specifically, Gerta warned me that I would have to bear some introductory bullying and harsh treatment by my peers, as I was a newcomer. However, I was lucky. The crowd had another target for this treatment at the same time as when I arrived.

One of the boys was assigned to take care of me, and he told me,

"Come with us, we are after Kohn."

"Why are you after him?" I asked.

"He is one of those Orthodox Jews," was the answer.

I was not sure what that meant, as I had only just started to realize what it meant to be an ordinary Jew. So it was strange to me that to be an Orthodox Jew should be a reason for giving somebody a bad time. However, it took the attention away from me as a newcomer, and so I joined the crowd. I wanted to find out what was going on, and I wanted to blend in with the group of my peers as fast as possible.

Well, the boys were hunting . . . They were running after a little boy who kept running away, jogging in the crowded corridor full of adults. The boy's problem was that he looked somewhat different from the other boys. He had glasses, he had longer hair than the other boys, and he had a little cap on his head that the other boys did not have. He was running away from us, and we were running after him and shouting something to tease him.

On the way, the boy who was supposed to take care of me showed me where the toilets and washrooms were. And, frankly, I considered this to be the most important and timely information at that time. It was definitely more important than the whole hunt for Kohn. The toilet was accessible from the corridor, not too far from the doors of our Heim. It was a facility common to all men in the vicinity, and there were lots of men, young and old, sometimes lining up to use the facility. There was a long trough made out of tin, and also the ordinary toilets and wash basins. It used to be a military facility, and was being run as such now.

Slowly I became used to this new life. I wanted to become a qualified member of the common gang. I wanted to belong. Gradually, I was losing the brand of being a newcomer. More and more I was becoming a qualified member. And so was everyone new, including Kohn.

Loneliness

It was with a lot of pain. I was lonely in the middle of a lot of children and strange adult people in a very crowded environment. I was on my own much too often, although my parents would visit me as often as they could. It was usually three or four times a week. Irene, my mom, had some privileges being a nurse in the hospital, as she had an irregular work schedule with night shifts. So she would come in the evening and bring some extra food for me. (And then she would go and visit my adopted brother with the same mission. I will say more of him later.) This was of course quite unpopular with my peers, and with the supervisors. My mom had to do it when everybody was supposed to be asleep already. But nobody was.

I learned the needed routines and local tricks as time passed by. Slowly, but more and more, I was becoming a qualified member of the gang. Of course I was just a commoner, not a member of the leading group, but this was all I was trying to achieve.

Gradually, I started to realize that I was one of the lucky ones. A lot of the children did not have parents around as I had. Their parents had already been sent by "working transport to the East," and they had to leave their children behind. Some parents made arrangements with relatives to take care of their children. Sometimes there were volunteers who temporarily "adopted" those children. It was a sad story. These "relatives" would visit the children occasionally only, mostly to punish them for bad behavior when invited to by our supervisors. Those children were practically without parental relationship, and naturally it was reflected in their behavior. Without knowing it for sure, the children were already orphans, and they felt it inside. Their substitution for the missing parental love was their strong friendship with each other. It was the ruling orphans' gang.

It took a lot of effort on my side, and a long time, to become a qualified member of the gang, although an orphan I was not, at least not yet. Then when I was accepted, it felt good to belong. We held together as much as we could, and covered up for each other. Life became less sad and more bearable for me. . .

And then, when I finally felt that I was a qualified member of the gang, my friends started to disappear. And the disappearance intensified rapidly when the end of the war was coming closer.

My Eternal Dream

"Hey Kids, kids: where are you going to?
Wait for me, wait for me. . ."

"We are leaving on a transport to the East. . .
We are leaving to the Place of No Return. . .
You will never see us again. . .
You stay back and remember us.
And you tell all the people. . ."

"I will, I will, I promise. . ."

I do. . .

The Vanishing Children

The percentage of orphans was growing as time progressed. More and more parents were sent by those cattle train "work" transports to the East. Then came the time when the orphans started to disappear into transports, "to join their parents." Practically, and as a result of the unofficial transport preference policy, the orphans were already on a death roll, as actually we all were. But some of us were not at the front of the line.

A pink sheet of paper with the name of the boy selected for the transport would appear in Hanka's hands, as delivered from the "Ghetto Self-Management Office." To tell the selected boy the bad news was one of Hanka's not too favorite duties. It would be formulated like he was selected to join his parents, who had left earlier, on a transport to the East.

Hanka would keep it very private, so other boys would not know about it. To spread the news or not was up to the boy himself. Hanka would help them to get ready, to pack up, and to wake them up early in the morning. They had to get to the assembly place on time. There were no farewell parties, no hugging, no kissing, not even a hand shake.

Mostly, we would not even notice the individual disappearing activity. The leaving boys would be careful not to wake us up. The commotion would only wake us up sometimes, when there was a larger group. Usually we would be surprised to see them leave, we would whisper some silly questions and whisper "goodbye," or "see you later," not to wake up the boys who were still sleeping. Mostly, we would just notice an empty bed in the morning. And we would try to move there if it was in a better location. Hanka would be the final authority on that bed changing activity.

Our "Crime" and Punishment

Our "crime" is that we were born Jews. According to the Nazis, the world had to be cleared free of us. From the Nazi point of view, their murdering method was actually a humanitarian act. Most of the victims of their "humanitarian act" were suffocated. Dying in the Nazi gas chambers took fifteen minutes. It was actually much less suffering, they said, than it takes the average citizen of this planet to die. What a murdering efficiency it was.

The bottom line was that our friends were fading away, one friend after another, and more often more than one at a time. New children were arriving, and some would go soon after their arrival. Finally, only a few of us survived. Practically, it was a race with time. How soon would the Nazi murdering machine collapse before the individual's turn to be murdered would come?

Our Everyday Life

Terezin concentration camp (or Theresienstadt Ghetto, as the Nazis called it) was a very people-concentrated place. After all, there were ten times more people there than the town was planned for. The streets were full of people all the time, and children were not supposed to be in the streets without parental or other adult supervision. The children in the Homes were actually in a prison within a larger prison, the concentration camp. However, whenever we managed to sneak out of the Heim and venture into the streets, we would be absorbed into the crowd and move along.

Most of the housing was in old blocks of apartment houses with separate common yards. Connections between the yards were made by openings in the dividing walls. The location of those connections was our secret knowledge. Using those connections, we could move around the town without many crossings of the streets. We would go to places where we were not supposed to be: manufacturing and maintenance shops, storage rooms, and such, and we would observe the adults' activities. Rarely would somebody would point out to us that we were not supposed to be there. We were getting street smart to Terezin standards, and we were trying to be as creative as the adults were in their quest for survival.

The most popular "professional" activity in our group was to be an electrician. The father of one of our friends was an electrical engineer by profession, and now he was on an electrical maintenance team. So one by one we would get some equipment like screw drivers and pliers, hammers, lighting equipment and wires. Somehow, we managed to have wooden boxes with front doors where we would hang all the treasures, and we would experiment with it all as well. (This was, of course later, near the end of our stay at Terezin, when the town was not so full anymore, and we were old buddies who had survived.)

Our New Heim

Our Heim moved several times, mostly for the better. We moved from our original location in the huge Dresden Barracks building into a building which used to be a post office originally. This building was located on a corner of the Main Square. The Main Square used to be a military parade field when Terezin was a military base. There was a large circus tent there now, and some military supplies for the Nazi army were produced there, using Terezin prisoners as workers. What was produced there was a secret, but general rumor had it that it was the production of gas masks.

This new room was more civilized in comparison with the military style of our previous location in the Dresden Barracks. There were larger windows, and there was a separate tower niche in one corner. Our new room was equipped with new bunk beds along the wall, and two rows down the center. However, the larger, private bunk beds for the supervisors were not ready when we moved in. Hanka and Erna were sleeping on upper beds along the wall. It just so happened that my bed was across the aisle from Hanka's bed, also on the upper level. Hanka issued an order in the morning to all the children to turn away from her so she could change. I was wondering what is she trying to hide, and so I invented a plan: I would pretend that I was not awake when she told us to turn away, and that I was just sleeping turned towards her bed. When I "woke up," I happened to open my eyes in the direction I was sleeping. Hanka did not buy it, and ordered me to turn the other way immediately, in a very angry tone. A separate niche in the tower was arranged for the supervisors that same day.

Hanka complained to my mother as soon as she came to visit me. My mom got very angry with me, and told me so in a very strong voice in front of Hanka. This was of course supposed to be for my own future benefit, as my mom and Hanka believed and told me. I should respect women's privacy, and avoid bad behavior in the future. I was very upset by this put-down, just because of my habit to explore the unknown! But nobody beat me up, so I should not complain too loudly.

Another little boy whose parents were gone in a transport was not so lucky. A grown up young man showed up one day in the afternoon at our Heim. I had never seen this man before. Suddenly, out of nothing, he took off his belt and started to chase the little boy, who ran from him and climbed under one of the bunk beds. It was pretty dusty under there, but the bed was lower than those for the adults, and the young man could not reach the little boy. The man started to shout at him to come out. The boy did not respond, and turned away from him, and kept shifting to increase the distance between them. I asked another boy nearby what this was all about. He told me this man was the boy's assigned volunteer adoptive uncle. He came to discipline the boy because Hanka called him. I asked what the boy did to deserve this. The response was that the little boy was picking his nose. So what? But he was eating it. I thought, he must have been hungry, or maybe he was after a desert.

Next to our Heim in the original Post Office building was the Terezin Ghetto Bank. It was there the famous but worthless Terezin Money was printed and distributed to Terezin prisoners.

The SS Nazi officers and guards were the most brutal and fanatic Nazi soldiers. They were given special tasks: they were guarding and managing the concentration camps of Nazi Germany. Their management office was called the SS Commandature. It was just across the square from our second Heim in the old Post Office. The Nazis also established a "Jewish Elders Self-Management Organization" so they could call the concentration camp a "Ghetto." However, the Jewish Elders were just given orders what to do, which was mostly directives stating how many prisoners should be prepared to fill the cattle train for the next transport. We could watch the SS guards through our windows when they were marching, or traveling in their automobiles to their workplace. We would look down on them from above, although we were not supposed to do this. But our Heim was located on the second floor, so practically speaking we could not avoid it.

The Nazis had a fence built around the streets they used, so they would not have to mix with the Jews. There were little gates made in the fence for Jews to cross. The gates were guarded by Jewish "policemen" in uniforms. They would let the Jews cross the Nazi-designated street only when no Nazis were in sight. One of those gates was just on the corner where our Heim Post Office building was. It was something to watch, and also to try occasionally!

Forbidden School

We were not to be educated at all, in accordance with the Nazi regulations. However, the Jews made an extreme effort to have their children educated despite the Nazi rules. They took a very dangerous risk in doing so. The punishment was simple: everybody involved would be allocated a place in the next transport to the East.

Practically speaking, this meant to be given a more advanced place on Death Row.

There were no official schools in Terezin at all. Our "school" was the Heim we lived in. The Jewish prisoners smuggled some educational books and other teaching items and learning aids into Terezin gradually, and the supplies grew steadily as time went by. The replenishment of new prisoners, due to steady allocations to transports to the East, increased the relative supply of teaching aids as well. We were sufficiently equipped, considering the circumstances.

We would just set up a blackboard and sit around our meal table after we finished our morning chores. Hanka would teach us the alphabet, and to read, write, and count. She would tell us stories from history and natural science. She would read to us in the evening, if we behaved. The practical result of all this effort was that I could enroll into a regular school class for my age after the end of the war, even though I had never been in a regular school before.

There were some close calls for the teaching activity as well. There was an inspection when we were located in the old Post Office building. A young SS officer with an entourage came to our Heim and looked around. There was a standing closet with shelves, covered in front with a drape instead of doors. The SS officer took his stick and moved the drape to look inside, to see if there were any books on the shelves. (He of course would not touch anything Jewish with his hands, even though he was wearing gloves.) He found nothing suspicious, and as far as we were concerned, the inspection was a success.

We had been given a warning ahead of the inspection, and we began cleaning and hiding things as soon as the warning came. Anything that could remotely imply a teaching activity was removed from the building, and this cleaning was rechecked several times. Rumor had it that a little boy from outside the Heim was seen walking with a typical school back pack (at that time it was a leather briefcase with straps) on his back. A policeman stopped him and asked where he was going. The wrong answer was "to school," and it was reported in writing. The report made its way to the top, and finally to the Commandature. The SS started to plan an inspection. However, a warning was sent by the Jewish Elders to all Heims as soon as the report started to move up the ranks. It actually ended up as a successful warning exercise. The Jewish "self-management" had to come up with some good explanation to the SS management, and it appeared they were successful that time. No special allocations to a transport were noted as a result of this incident.

Games

The most popular sport action in Terezin was soccer. It was played in the barracks yards, because there was no actual soccer field available. The yards were smaller than an ordinary soccer field, so teams were reduced in size from eleven to seven. One advantage of playing in the barracks yards was that there were two stories of an open balcony all the way around the yards, which were used as an observation place to watch the games. There was a soccer league competition, followed very enthusiastically by many. It was easy for us to watch the games by just walking to the balcony outside our big doors, due to the favorable location of the Heim. The barracks had three yards connected by the open balconies, and the soccer games were played mostly in the center yard.

We children would also play soccer sometimes for fun and physical exercise. We did not have a real soccer ball, so we would use some small, handmade balls, usually socks filled with bits of old rugs. I myself was not too good at soccer, so my parents arranged with my uncle Frank, my father's cousin, to train me occasionally. Frank was one of the soccer players who was sort of a local star, so it was a great privilege for me to have him as a personal coach. Uncle Frank would take me out on top of the fortifications where there were open grassy spaces, and he would train me to play using "professional" kicks, and all the tricks. It did not improve my performance too much physically, but it definitely improved my image as a soccer player with my peers, at least for a while.

Another game was to prove one's courage, for example to touch a dead human body. The main hospital where my mom worked provided some opportunities. I would go to visit my mother at her working and living place in the hospital almost every second day, in the afternoon. The hospital personnel would put the bodies in a dark space under the staircase, to be picked up for transportation to the Crematorium outside the Terezin concentration camp permitted boundaries. Our game was to climb in the dark space under the stairs where the dead body was lying, and touch the dead face. It was scary for us, and it was not permitted by any camp rules, especially by Jewish religious rules. The one who touched the dead body the most was the winner. I don't remember ever winning this game.

Carrying the Remains

Occasionally we would be involved in some light work we were thought to be able to do. One of these occasions was to help in the disposing of the never ending rows of cardboard boxes filled with ashes of those who had died in Terezin.

We would be led outside the boundaries of the permitted area, to the Columbarium. It was actually a simple storage area with shelves in one of the old fortification structures. There were rows of gray cardboard boxes on the shelves. Each of those boxes had a nicely written name on it, including the birth and death dates of the person whose ashes were presumed to be in the box. Some of the children would say, "If you see my grandmother's box, with the name of such and such on it, set it aside for me. But this never happened. There were too many boxes. The columbarium was emptied quite frequently, and there was some official supervision by an SS officer as well.

We would take the cardboard boxes with the ashes from the shelves, organize a chain of children, and load the boxes on the carts prepared outside the fortress building. The carts were actually old Jewish funeral carriages with the top cut off, to be used for transportation of various loads in Terezin. So, after all, they were quite appropriate for this occasion, as it was supposed to be the last trip of the deceased. The carts were pushed by Terezin Jewish prisoners instead of pulled by horses as they would be under normal circumstances.

All the boxes were taken to a river outside the fortress, where they were thrown in, to make space for the new ones. This ash to river throwing was actually a quite frequent activity, considering the amount of daily ash production in the Terezin Crematorium. Death in Terezin was a routine everyday happening: people somehow were used to it.

Death in the Field

It was on 11 November 1943, the 25th anniversary of Germany's defeat in World War I. The Nazis believed that the Jews were Germany's internal and external Enemy Number 1. The Jews were supposed to be responsible for Germany's defeat. The Jews were also supposed to be responsible for the enforced Versailles Peace Treaty, which was very harsh on Germany. And the Jews, they said, were also responsible for all Germany's internal and external problems. According to Adolph Hitler, the final goal was a total removal of all the Jews from Germany, from Europe, and from the world.

Once again, on this anniversary, the Nazis had to get even with their Enemy Number 1, at least in Terezin. On that day, the Nazi management assembled almost all the 47,000 prisoners at that time on a large, square field outside the camp limits. The census, the body count, lasted for 18 hours in a cold rain. Many of the prisoners died during the census, or soon after.

Irene, my mom, came to our Heim in her white nurse's uniform early in the morning on that day. She declared that I was ill, and that she had to take me to the hospital where she worked, right now. And she did.

Presently we arrived at the hospital, and we went directly to a large patients' room full of probably 30 beds. All the beds were fully occupied with patients. Apparently my mom had arranged with one old patient to share his bed with me, and he did. I had to sit while he was lying, and he sat while I was lying. There was no physician's morning inspection that day. An SS officer in a perfect uniform and with a notebook came instead. He was counting the patients, including me, and did not say a word. So nobody had to explain anything. The officer seemed to be in a hurry to get it done, and to get out of the hospital as fast as he could. He obviously did not appreciate his visiting duty in a hospital full of Jews, most likely infested with dangerous diseases.

I had survived another challenge. But the way I did it did not help improve my luck of popularity with my buddies. Nobody wanted to talk about their census experience when I asked. They told me much later how they survived by holding together. They were cold and hungry out there in the field. They did not have any toilets, including our lady supervisors. Again, they had to form their bodies into a ring, and turn to face outside the ring, when the supervisors had to do their needs. Somebody told me later that the Nazis had a very noisy military airplane flying low over the field above their heads to scare them. They were afraid that airplanes were flying in to shoot them or drop some bombs on them.

The children, and all other prisoners, had to be organized into square groups of 25, and the SS officers counted the groups in one row and then the next. They did this several times, apparently always with a different result. (Most likely mathematics was not their strong subject.) That night they gave up, and the prisoners could return back in a not too well organized retreat. It was late in the night when all the children made it back to the Heim. They fell on their beds completely exhausted, but happy that they had made it back, all of them.

The Girl in the Children's Hospital

There was a children's hospital located near our Heim, in the Post Office building. I was a frequent visitor there. Luckily the illnesses were never too severe, a common cold or flu was sufficient to justify my relocation to the hospital. Actually, in those days a simple cold was a more serious illness than it is today. Penicillin was not available, and all other medicines were in short supply. Just to get ill was a scary event. My mom would move me from my Heim to this hospital whenever there was a suspicion of sickness. Her work position as a nurse in the main hospital would be a help, of course. Everybody had some privileges, and this was hers.

Once, near the beginning of our stay, two of my mom's aunts came to visit me when I was in the children's hospital again with the flu. They brought some little goodies for me to eat, and they asked if I would eat this, knowing I was a picky eater. I answered "I will eat everything," and they started to cry, "Oh, the poor child, he eats everything." However, soon after this incident they disappeared to the "East," not to be seen again. Only this little story was what remained with me.

The last time I was moved once again to this children's hospital, due to some sickness suspicion, stands out quite vividly in my mind even to today. This was in the times of high transportation activity. Next to me in the bed was a girl sick with a cold, probably the same as I was. We talked, and I learned that she was one of those children selected for the next transport. She was living with her mother, not in a Heim like I was. She and her mother were supposed to leave the next day with a transport to the East. She was one year older than me, so she was probably nine years old at the time. Her name was Elaine, I believe.

Not being the most tactful child, I asked her how does it feel to be selected to die. She was not shocked too much by this question, as it was actually quite a real possibility. Her answer surprised me: "What shall be, shall be." This was something I had never heard from my parents, or from my supervisors in the Heim.

I asked her if she would do something about it. She said there was nothing to do about it. I suggested that she could disappear in the streets, and hide somewhere until the transport was gone. Her answer was that someone else would just have to go in her place. In addition, there might be a real possibility they would meet her father there, as he was transported to the East earlier. But it was obvious she did not believe that would be a real possibility.

We talked about a lot of other things, of course, as young boys and girls do, and it lasted into the night. The girl was gone in the morning when I woke up, and I never saw her again.

I have thought about her quite often since that incident in the hospital. What if she told her mother about our talk when she came to pick her up for the transport? Maybe she convinced her mother to go and hide. Or maybe her mother already had that planned. Maybe her mother would have told the little girl, "What do you think you are in the hospital for? It was part of my plan to disappear into the overcrowded maze of the Terezin concentration camp."

The reality was that children leaving for transport had their own particular feeling they were among those who would most likely die. Going to the East meant going to a place from which nobody had yet returned. There was no general knowledge in Terezin of the gas chambers in the "East places" at that time. However, the official statement that the children were going to join their parents (or their father, if they were traveling with their mother) was accepted only with great suspicion.

The New Train Line

There was a major construction project in Terezin in 1943: the construction of approximately three miles of a railway spur connecting Terezin with the main line in Bohusovice. That was the place where we arrived on our train trip from Prague. From there, we walked the last three miles. The official explanation for the new spur was that it would make the shipments of supplies to and from Terezin easier. At that time, remember, there was a big tent factory erected in the main square in front of the church. The factory products were gas masks, per our gang information network. So it seemed to be quite reasonable to have a railway line for the factory shipments.

As far as the real purpose of the spur: Rumor had it that the new rail connection was built to make the transports to Terezin, and mainly from Terezin to the East, more efficient. And efficiency was something the Nazis were always proud to be associated with.

The construction activity was an interesting show for us, although we could watch only the small part which took place inside the boundaries of the concentration camp. However, there was more than just a show to it when the construction of the spur was completed and the engines began to bring closed freight wagons into the town. The line had several endings right on one of the streets, and was accessible from the pavement for anybody, including us. We would jump on the wagon platforms and enjoy the ride when the engines moved the wagons from one line to another. There were big bangs as the engines kicked the wagons and connected them to the train. This lasted for a while, and we had free rides. For us kids this was an ultimate adventure for some time.

It ended when we were told by our Heim supervisors about an encounter a little boy had with an SS officer. The little boy was on a wagon platform expecting to have a free ride, as was our common practice. The SS appeared from nowhere and hit the boy in the face so strongly that the boy fell down, flying from the platform onto the pavement, and was badly hurt. The boy woke up in the Children's Hospital, and did not remember too much. We remembered not to climb on those wagons anymore. It might have been an efficient rumor sent out by the Jewish "self-government committee," or it might have been a fact. In any event, we took it seriously. So for a while the new railway line and the trains provided some entertainment for us, the little inhabitants of Terezin concentration camp. It was something like a ferry ride for children who were outside the walls of the camp.

The rumor about the real purpose of the new railway line connection turned out to be correct. Big waves of transports materialized in 1944. It cleaned out the Terezin population in a big way. In the eyes of the children, the overcrowded concentration camp changed into an almost empty ghost town. For those whose family members disappeared, the emptiness was overwhelming.

For the Nazis, it was an important part of their murdering machine. It provided additional efficiency and secrecy. The prisoners on their way to their ultimate destination were getting there faster and in a discreet manner. They were not seen anymore being loaded into the cattle wagons at the Bohusovice public railway station, or carrying their belongings those three miles to or from Terezin. Nobody could guess for sure what was inside each cattle wagon.

For the prisoners, specifically for those selected for immediate transport, it was a matter of "what shall be, shall be. . ."

The allocations for transport to the east caught up with Paul, my father, in the fall of 1944. It was a very sad story for us, as we did not know if we would ever see him again. Everybody at that time was sure that the end of the war was close. However there had been no returns from the "East," at least not yet. All we could do was hope for the best. And that was what mom and I, Irene and Tommy, did. However, within the gang of my peers, I was qualified as half an orphan as soon as my father left. I grew in rank, but this was a poor compensation for missing a father.

Only a remembrance was left with us. We would remember how his spirit was always high, expecting the end of the war at any time soon; how he would talk about every cultural performance in Terezin, and how the performers kept vanishing in the transports; how he took me to the Brundibar children's opera in the attic of one of the barracks. He was gone now, and we did not know if we would ever see him again.

~~~

Tommy's Father, Paul, in front of his childhood home in Domazlice, where he was born 8 August 1904

Tommy in Schwanenbruckel, two years old, July 1938.

Four year old Tommy on skis in Radesovice, near Prague, January 1941.

Five year old Tommy in his Tatra Automobile in Radesovice, near Prague, 1941.

Tom's Family: Bela, Uncle Fred and Tommy, Tommy's Father (Paul), and Uncle Pavu (Paul).

Family and Friends. Top: Rosl Abeles, Pavel Spitz, Olga Spitz, Irene Lustig, Gertrude Abeles, Paul Lustig. Bottom: Ruth Abeles, Tommy Lustig.

The last Three Miles to Terezin. For us, September 1942

New Transport Entering Terezin

Our New Life In The Attic.

Tommy's First Home, Second Floor, Dresden Barracks.
Picture Taken 2005.

Hospital Barracks Where Tommy's Mother, Irene, Lived.
Picture Taken 2005.

Main Entrace to the Hospital Where Irene Worked.
Picture Taken 2005.

Drawing of a Typical Building Block Courtyard.

Soccer Game in Dresden Barracks Courtyard.
Corridor Bleachers.

Our Second Home, the Old Post Office, the Windows on the
Second Floor Were Ours. Picture taken 2005.

SS Commandature, in the Old Bank Building.
Picture Taken May, 2005

Terezin Columbarium, Where We Carried the Ashes.
Picture taken in May 2005

Tommy's Third Home, the Old School Building.
Picture taken in May 2005

Terezin Liberation.
May, 1945.

The Old Gate, Where My Father "Organized a Private Transportleitung Office." The Gate Was Closed Permanently at that Time. Picture taken 2005.

My Father in Front of His Military Unit Barracks in
Moravska Ostrava, Hranecnik, June, 1945.

Tommy, at His Father's Military Unit Barracks in
Moravska Ostrava, Hranecnik, June, 1945.

Tom's Holocaust Presentation at a Seattle School.

Pavel's Violin

Chapter Five
My Father's Odyssey

My Father Leaves

My father disappeared into one of the last big transports of autumn 1944. Although he believed to the last minute, as everybody did, that he would be excluded, off he went. Everybody had believed that he would be excluded, because of his importance to the wellbeing and functioning of the Terezin camp, the "Ghetto" as the Nazis called it. Or because of his connection to the people in the Ghetto Self Management Organizaton, or of his position in the community, and so on. However, one by one (or actually thousands by thousands) ultimately everyone had to go to satisfy the needs of the Nazi war machinery. And more importantly, as we learned later, to satisfy the needs of the commitment to the final solution of the Jewish problem. The final solution turned out to be the total extermination of the Jewish race. The Nazis at that time started to collect Jewish artifacts from all over occupied central Europe to create museums in Prague of the (recently) extinct Jewish race.

The nature of the extermination plan, the so-called "Final Solution," was not known at that time inside Terezin. Officially,the transports were work transports. Sometimes family members were transported to the East to "join" the family members already there. Ironically this was not a lie, specifically when the family members to be joined had already been murdered. And this was actually the prevailing case. At that time it was already clear that the transports to the East were a road of no return. This was at a time when the outcome of the war was already obvious, with Nazi Germany mostly gone as we knew it. However, the Nazis did not see it that way. They were trying to change events by increasing the production of needed war supplies. Accordingly, the transports were officially called transports to work camps ("Lagers.")

The people were loaded into cattle trains right inside Terezin now. There was the new railway line, so conveniently built to make this process really efficient. The travel conditions were not too cozy inside the cattle trains, even in comparison to the crowded conditions inside Terezin. The cattle train was more than full of people of different ages and attitudes. There was no toilet, just a bucket which was handed out at infrequent stops, when and if the guards opened the door. There were no benches in the wagon. So the prisoners had to stand, or sit on the floor, if there was some space. They took turns to sit and stand.

My father and his close friend, Aaron, got really angry with the Nazis for treating them this way, like animals. My father and his friend and of course all the others in the cattle train were frustrated, and promised each other that they would never again work for the Nazis at all, because the Nazis really did not deserve the benefit of their labor.

Obviously the crowded conditions on the train did not make the people too polite to each other. There were some nasty, uncivilized moments between the cattle car inhabitants. Pleasantries were not what they used to be as the conditions on the trip became less and less comfortable, less and less bearable. Not only did the full bucket, their only toilet, contribute to the atmosphere, but also the lack of space for sitting, the lack of food, and the general tension. Nobody knew what to expect at the end of the journey. So the friends tried to keep up high spirits.

Aaron would say, "The Germans must definitely be dumb and crazy if they expect to get some meaningful work out of all these people when they are treating them like this."

"Yeah," added Paul, "They have a lot to learn if they expect to be in charge of the world for the next 1,000 years."

They definitely did not lose their black humor. But they were not prepared for the surprising facts of life presented to them at the end of the journey.

The train slowed.

"At last we are at the end of our trip," someone said. "I hope they will open the door and take out this bucket!"

"It definitely was not the most pleasant journey of my life," said Paul, not knowing how close it would come to really being his last journey.

"Although the company was mostly pleasant after all," Aaron replied sarcastically.

Auschwitz, The Extermination Camp

The train finally stopped and a guard slid the door

open. He started to shout,

"Get the hell out of there, we do not have the whole day! Hurry up and line up here!"

Paul said, "I agree this time. There is not much more I would like to do either. Let's get the hell out of this stinking coffin!" and he jumped down onto the already crowded platform

There were a lot of people on the muddy platform. There were also some local people from the huge concentration camp. They came to collect the belongings, which were in a separate wagon. The locals were all dressed in striped uniforms, like real inmates. This was shocking news to the newcomers. They suddenly realized that they would be real prisoners from then on. There was a lot of shoving and pushing. The new arrivals were an unorganized mass of people, somehow progressively pushed in one direction, toward where the exit probably was. The two friends, Paul and Aaron, got separated. Suddenly everybody was on their own destiny, and everyone was looking around to see what the new environment was. There were fences and fences and fences, with barbed wire on the top. And in this, all the mass of people were moving ahead, forward to their unknown destination. The driving force was everybody's desire to get this over with, and to settle down somewhere else.

Somebody was shouting, "Hey, Mr. Lustig, report yourself as young and healthy, and willing to work!"

Paul was thinking about this, and it all somehow

became clear to him at once: this place was not just a work camp. He frantically began trying to get this message to his friend Aaron, but he could not reach him. The mass of people was moving ahead like a rushing river. As Paul looked around, trying to reach his friend, the stream of people formed a narrow line, with the help of some not too gentle guards.

One by one the newcomers appeared before an SS officer. This was the famous Doctor Joseph Mengele, the "Man of Destiny." He, who faced everybody, did not talk. He listened, looked, and then pointed with his thumb to the right or to the left, depending upon his judgment of the usefulness of each individual standing in front of him. There was some work to be done for the Fatherland. However, there was also an extermination plan for the Jews, the Final Solution project. And a daily quota had to be reached as well. Unknowingly, Paul was lucky with his appearance and his changed attitude. This time he made it, and his friend did not. He never forgot about that, and blamed himself for not getting the message to Aaron. So the trip to the work camp, the trip to Auschwitz, ended with a life or death selection. My father Paul, thanks to an unknown friend's warning, reported himself as healthy and willing to work, and this saved his life for the time being. However, this was the end of just one chapter, and the beginning of another journey. There were many more close calls to come.

Paul's transport designation was EM. It left Terezin on 1 October 1944. There were 1,500 prisoners on this transport, 1,000 men and 500 women. Of these, 370 men and 60 women were selected to live. The rest were sent to the gas chambers right after their arrival, right from the selection ramp. After the war, there were 306 survivors from this transport out of the 430 selected to live.

It came to Paul at that moment, when his unknown friend shouted his warning to him, that this was all about survival. The end of the war was surely not too far off. This was actually the belief from the start, from the day we arrived at Terezin. However, now the armies from the east and from the west were closing in on the Nazis in rapid progress. The only chance to survive was to hold on to your life and keep up hope. Just keep watching the light at the end of the tunnel, and don't lose it from your focus.

Whatever It Takes to Survive . . .

This is a jungle, the name of which is Auschwitz labor camp. But actually it is a Death Camp. Although the Nazis have written above every possible gate, *"Arbeit Macht Frei*, Work Makes You Free." *My foot it makes . . . but, let's hang on to it.*

The disinfecting process, tattoo on the forearm, and the exchange of civilian clothing for the striped prison uniforms, came first. The showers actually produced water for those considered fit to do some work for the Nazis. (For most of the newcomers, there were openings in the roof above the showers, and the SS dropped some powder, Zyklon-B, on them through the openings to produce poison gas. Then they shut the openings. It took about 15 minutes for everyone to die of suffocation. (What a humanitarian murdering method it was.)

Boots and shoes were exchanged for inmate's slippers. Paul had a pair of nice Canada boots on him when he arrived, and he really wanted to keep them. As it turned out, his foot size was too small and there were no slippers available that fit him. So, after some negotiation, he got his Canada boots back. It was definitely one of the lucky omens, he believed. It saved his life on the death march which came later, at the end of his time at Auschwitz. Finally, the prisoners were assigned to spaces in the barracks.

Paul's Accounting Skills at Use

The prisoners were taken to their new workplace the next day. It was in the attached production facilities. Nobody knew what they produced. It turned out the German supervisor in charge of the department Paul was assigned to was not too proficient in accounting. So after he discovered Paul had an accounting background, he selected Paul to do his accounting for him. It was a great risk for Paul, for he had to succeed in cleaning up the accounting mess. He did, and the German supervisor appreciated it, and kept Paul alive with an extra bread sandwich occasionally. This was a great help, though Paul had to eat it in secret. However, he could share his regular watery soup with others sometimes, as long as it did not create suspicion.

The Hungry Newcomer

A young newcomer was very hungry, and he ate another prisoner's soup while the other had turned away. This was a very bad act, and could be punished with death if reported. Paul convinced the offended prisoner to accept his own soup instead, and not report it to the SS. It took some negotiation, as the one who had lost his soup was very angry. But finally he agreed to eat Paul's soup, and forget about the incident.

Many years later, after the war, Paul was walking along a crowded street in downtown Prague. Suddenly, someone jumped out of the crowd and started to hug a very surprised Paul, shouting,

"Thank you, Paul, you saved my life! I was looking for you all these years to meet you and thank you! Now I can die in peace. . ."

Keep the Spirit High . . .

It was very important to keep as high a spirit as possible in the barracks. It was not only the lack of sufficient food, but also other nuisances like bed bugs and fleas. This became really bad, and bothered everyone. One Sunday, Paul organized a cleaning day for his barracks. Everyone took out all their infested belongings to be thrown away. Most importantly, they washed themselves completely. This was quite an exercise, as the weather was freezing, and only cold water was available. But afterwards all the friends living in the barracks felt much better, and the sinking spirit was lifted again.

Getting a New Coat

From time to time there were calls for volunteers for special working crews to do work outside of the camp. The general psychology was that it was good to get into those crews to get out of the camp, assuming the working conditions would be better. So there was always a big rush to get on the list, as people were selected on a first come first served basis.

On one occasion Paul got on one of those lists. This was associated with being given new uniforms. The group lined up in the yard. Paul was standing there in his new outfit, feeling somewhat uncomfortable. The clerk in the uniform storage was in a hurry, so he gave Paul whatever came to his hand first. Paul's friends looked at him and told him to go back and get it changed, as the new coat was definitely too big. Paul went back to the storeroom and haggled with the clerk to have the coat exchanged for a smaller one. This took some time, and when Paul came back the group had already gone. Paul was very upset, blaming himself and everyone else for losing this opportunity to get outside the camp, just because of an ill-fitting coat. Well, at least he could keep the clean new outfit.

After some time he started to appreciate the new coat more and more. None of those volunteers ever returned to the camp, and they were never heard from again. It was just another death trap, and good luck for Paul.

The End Is Near

The time was moving slowly. Everyone was expecting the end of the war soon. That was the hope of the survivors, but more and more people were dying from lack of food, exhaustion, and mostly loss of hope, loss of a sense of life.

Paul was watching the new transport arrivals, through the barbed wire fence. The transports to Terezin were now mostly women with little chidren. Dr. Mengele's selection for work had become much simpler. The women with children were chosen for death almost without exception. They were directed straight to the shower chambers with gas supplied instead of water. And Paul saw, in his imagination, so many times his wife Irene with little Tommy, his son, lining up there. In this Paul was not alone, for so did lots of others who had left their wives and children in Terezin concentration camp. Now they were all hanging onto life by going about their routine almost automatically: work, eat, and as much sleep as they could get.

Death March

Near the end of 1944, the Nazis started to prepare for the liquidation of the camp. Obviously, the prisoners were afraid the Nazi guards would murder them all before leaving. But the plan turned out to be much different. When the guards left the camp, they took the prisoners with them. They organized Death Marches (*"Todesmarchen."*) Prisoners by the thousands were marched to the west, toward Germany, in the cold and snows of January 1945. Those who could not keep up, or fell, were shot to death on the spot. Paul's small feet, and the Canada boots he had managed to save for himself, saved his life this time for sure.

The prisoners on Paul's march (there were many others) were led further west into another camp already emptied, and were left there. The Red Army progress was faster than the Death March, so the prisoners were abandoned in the new camp, and the guards ran away. Luckily, the guards did not shoot the prisoners first, as had happened elsewhere.

In the Middle of Battle

The Nazi German army was on the west of the camp, and the Red army on the east. Soon the battle started, and for several days the armies were exchanging intense fire, with the camp and the prisoners in the middle. The shells were flying above their heads; they were in no-man's-land. The Nazi guards seemed to have disappeared completely. There had not been too much food when they arrived in the camp, and after a while there was no food at all.

The prisoners were hungry, and started to search the camp. Paul, with a small group, searched the area near the barracks, and then they ventured further, to a high wooden fence. They decided to climb the fence, and as Paul was getting ready to be the first one over a younger friend stopped him and told him not to.

"You, Paul, still have hope to get back to your family," he said. "They may still be alive. I know for sure I don't have anybody left anymore. I'll go."

And off he went to the top of the fence, with the others giving him support and a push. The minute he was on top, a shot cracked, and he fell down dead. Everybody was shocked, and the rest of the group ran back to the barracks for cover. Paul realized with a shock that the dead one could have been himself, and that he was lucky once again.

The armies were still standing on opposite sides of the camp, not moving yet, but only occasionally exchanging fire. The prisoners became more and more motivated by hunger. So after a while they ventured out again, hoping the Nazi guards had run away by now. But they were still scared, and afraid to take any unnecessary risk. They decided to dig a tunnel under the fence. That way they would not have to show themselves above the fence and make an easy target.

The prisoners used their eating utensils as tools. This time it was Paul who went first, and, luckily, no shots were fired. Five others followed after him, and they started to explore the part of the camp that was outside the first fence.

Escape at Last

But the prisoners did not find any food at all. They did find a store room full of galvanized cooking utensils, army issue. Presently they thought out a plan: They would take as many of the utensils as they could carry, and they would go to a nearby Polish village. They would exchange them for some food and some old clothing. (They were afraid to walk around in their striped prison uniforms, because they expected to be a target for Nazi guards again. Some of them might still be around.) And so they just walked out of the camp, and for the first time, they were free!

The nearest Polish farm village was actually not too far. The prisoners decided to split into three teams of two each, and they walked to the village. Paul and his partner selected a medium sized house, and they entered.

Their plan worked, at least partly. The Polish villagers did not have too much spare food or clothing to give. However, the shiny utensils were a good bargain for a little food, and they were willing to help the hungry as well. But the villagers were scared of the Nazis, so they gave the prisoners what they wanted and hurried them out and away.

In the meantime the armies were still exchanging fire, with the concentration camp and most of the prisoners in the middle. Paul never saw any of them again, nor the other four who escaped with him.

Paul Joins the Army

Paul and his partner figured out that the Red Army would be east of where they were. At least that was the direction where some of the firing was coming from. Off they went. They had to walk for quite some time, and hide on the way. They had civilian clothes on them now, but they also still had their tattoos with their prisoner number still on their arms. Actually, they never got rid of those tattoos.

Finally, they reached the Red Army, and told them they wanted to join. The Red Army was very well experienced with this situation already. First they provided soup, the same way they were feeding their soldiers. Immediately after that they moved Paul and his companion to a cleaning unit. Almost all the prisoners liberated from the nearby concentration camps were infested with lice and fleas. It created a health risk for them, and for everyone who came in contact with them.

About two days later Paul and his partner were told they could not stay with the Red Army. This was because they were free Czechoslovakian citizens again. They were told there was a Czech Army unit attached to the Red Army, and they were transported to that unit's headquarters. For the first time since leaving on the Terezin transport from Prague in 1942, Paul was at last among free Czechs.

The unit was looking for Czech volunteers who would like to join them. Paul saw an opportunity to get even with the Nazis. He reasoned that the Nazis did so much bad to the people of Europe, specifically to the Jews, and namely his family; though he did not know the full extent of the Nazi crimes yet. Paul had imagined so many times his wife Irene and his son Tommy in the line for death in the gas chambers in Auschwitz, that he was sure they were dead by now. He felt he should do his part to help return freedom to the people still in the grip of the Nazis. The Nazis were not defeated, not yet. They were still doing so much harm to others.

Paul had never had any military training like most male citizens used to have in the prewar Czechoslovakia. He wore glasses, and this had been good enough to be excused from the mandatory two years of military training. However, glasses were not a good reason for not enlisting recruits during a war. He could drive an automobile. Truck drivers were needed mostly to supply the fighters with ammunition and other needed supplies. Although he had never driven a truck, Paul got enlisted in no time. He was given the needed truck driver training and the basic boot camp training "on the job."

Presently, Paul was assigned to the automobile transportation unit. This unit had a great tradition in combat. After the war, Paul's comrades from the unit would tell me stories of how they were under heavy enemy fire, supplying Russian and Czech combat units, mainly artillery, with trucks overloaded with ammunition, up the steep and slippery hills in the Carpathian Mountains. Those were scary stories full of excitement, and also some humor, sometimes with tragic endings.

It came up after Paul had already been with the unit for some time that they were looking for a "pep-talker" to keep the fighting spirit of the unit high. Paul was a man of contagious enthusiasm. He was known to be able to keep the morale of his comrades high in any situation. He would not miss any opportunity to tell his fellow soldiers about the horrors the Nazis did not only to the Jews, but to everybody whom they disliked. He would explain that the Nazis had to be defeated with the greatest effort possible, and as soon as possible. And, most importantly, he himself was indeed highly motivated to fight. In addition, he knew a lot about the culture, democratic tradition, and spirit of prewar Czechoslovakia. He was also a skilled musician. He played the violin best. So he was soon assigned the post of "Cultural Officer," although he was not a commissioned officer as far as military rank was concerned. Promotion to officer, first lieutenant, came later, at the time of his demobilization.

~~~

Chapter Six
Uncle Fred

The Partisans

The partisans called it *Štrbska Hut*, high in the Tatra Mountains in the dense woods above *Štrbska Pleso* (Lake,) in the northern extension of the Carpathian Mountain Ring. It was the Štrbska Partisan group's hidden survival hut. It served well when the times were not too good. And the times were not too good after the Slovak National Uprising was brutally crushed.

The hut was partly also a recuperation place for the wounded. However, there was a shortage of medical supplies, food, and good spirits most of the time. The wounded did not have too much chance of survival if their wound was of a serious nature. To discuss the survival chances of the rest of them was not a favored topic either.

The partisans would venture out when the rain or snow occasionally stopped, and they would talk about their hopes for the future. Fred had changed his name to Jiri (George) Rastislav Lenda. Periodic name changes had been a necessary part of the routine for him ever since he joined the Slovak underground at the end of 1942. During the long nights at Štrbska Hut he would see his girlfriend, Bela, in his dreams. Rastislav, or "Rasti" as they called him, was dreaming about getting back to liberated Prague, marrying his beloved Bela, and restarting his physician practice as he had left it.

Decades after the war, his beloved Bela would bring his ashes up to this spot, high in the Tatras, accompanied by Rasti's surviving friend, Žikeš. They would spread the ashes around, not talking much, each immersed in their own thoughts and remembering their common fight for freedom and, finally, for survival.

Brothers Leaving Prague

"See you again at the clock at six after the war" were the last words my father, mother and I heard from my Uncle Fred before we were transported by train to the Terezin concentration camp. This was actually a popular saying borrowed partly from a famous Czech book, *The Good Soldier Svejk*, referencing World War I and his favorite pub in the story. This time the reference was to the Clock which used to be at the top of Wenceslas Square. It was the most common dating and meeting place in prewar Prague. The Clock is long gone by now, but the Square is still a popular meeting place.

It was a show of bravado on my uncle's part. He was supposed to be on the same transport to Terezin as we were. But he did not show up at the designated assembly place at the Prague Exhibition Hall. Instead, he came to the platform at the railway station from which the train was leaving, just to say goodbye to us.

Fred escaped to Slovakia over the eastern border late in winter. Slovakia was a separate state at that time. Officially, Slovakia was an ally of Hitler's "Third Reich."

Escape to Slovakia was not an easy task. Fred had

to obtain false personal documents for a new identity first. He traveled by train to the eastern border of the then Third Reich Protectorate of Bohemia and Moravia (now the Czech Republic.) Disguised as a tourist skier, he hiked along the top of the Beskydy Mountains, along the border. There he met a border guard, who checked his documents and let him go. Then, instead of going back to the Czech side, Fred skied down the Slovakian side. The border guard whistled at him, but did not shoot, and Fred vanished into the tree line.

There was no Slovak guard at the top to stop him as he skied down the hills into Slovakia. He got to the bottom safely, ditched his skis in a little creek and changed from his ski outfit into civilian hiking clothes. He shaved, and improved his general appearance from supplies in his back pack. Then he buried everything he had carried with him, and proceeded further on foot.

At the bottom of the valley he walked into a little village and met a Slovakian policeman. The policeman checked his identity documents. The documents Fred showed him were different from those he had presented to the Czech-Moravia border guard. The Slovakian policeman found the new documents in order, and then he asked Fred, now Dr. Rastislav Hála, whether he had seen anyone fitting his former description. Obviously the Czech guard had alerted the Slovak authorities to be on the lookout for him.

The Slovak Underground Resistance

Shortly after his arrival, my Uncle Fred joined the Slovak anti-Nazi underground resistance. His new identity was Dr. Jiri (George) Rastislav Gala. He started to work as a fund raiser for the resistance organization. This was dangerous work, as there was always the possibility of a trap, although the German Gestapo was not overly active in Slovakia at the time. However, there was an active Slovak state police, affiliated with the Slovak Nazi-sympathetic government. Luckily, the members of the state police were highly flexible, and very pragmatic. They preferred immediate material rewards to the political principles of the Nazis.

Many of the local Slovak entrepreneurs made some good money participating in the war economy. To do this, they had to show support for the local government, which was friendly towards Hitler's Germany. However, at the time of Rastislav's fund raising activity, the war situation had changed and was no longer too promising for Germany. The practical and rational Slovak entrepreneurs were now eager to demonstrate that they were ready to support the Allies' side, so that the Slovak nation could be freed from the Nazi collaborating government.

In addition, Rasti, and his fiancée, Bela, worked as couriers between the Czech and the Slovak underground organizations. The Czech underground had to communicate with the Exile Czechoslovakian Government in London to let them know about the status of subversive action preparations. More importantly, the Czech underground had to let the Exile Government in London know details about their readiness to receive and hide the parachuted ammunition supplies and, sometimes, parachuted military personnel. But they could not communicate by radio transmission from Czech territory, as the Gestapo was very active there, and had the ability to trace down the location of radio transmissions quite successfully. This was in general not the case in the Slovak state territory, specifically the Tatra Mountains where the partisans were hiding out were almost completely free from Nazi control at the time. Bela, who was a gynecologist and lived in Prague, would receive the coded messages and travel with them to the Czech-Slovak border. She and Fred would meet at a popular mountain border lodge called Bumbálka. Bela would give the coded messages to Rasti (Fred,) and he would take them to the Slovak partisans for radio transmission to London.

However, there were some tight experiences as well. One night, when Bela arrived at the border meeting place at Bumbálka Lodge, an SS officer suddenly appeared as she and Rasti were walking together outside the lodge. The SS officer put his arms around them both in a friendly manner, and joined them in their walk. This scared Bela to death. She was thinking, "This is it. I am going to be taken to the interrogation room right now. I will be tortured and I will end up in one of the Nazi prisons waiting for execution." To her surprise, Rasti introduced the SS officer to her as a close friend of his.

Later, Rasti explained to Bela that this officer (as well as many others) had been bribed by the Slovak underground. Now the SS officer was helping the underground by looking the other way, as long as there was a continuous supply of money. The system seemed to work quite reliably: The German Army was paying the Slovak entrepreneurs generously for their products and services. Then, part of the money ended up in the underground coffers, and part of it ended up back in the pockets of German soldiers and other officials. It appeared to be a well-functioning, rational economic system. The Nazis were in fact paying for a well-organized fight against themselves!

The Slovak National Uprising

Rasti joined the Slovak partisans when the Slovak National Uprising became a reality. Slovakia was proclaimed to be again a part of the new Czechoslovakia, in the northern Slovak town of Banska Bistryce in the fall of 1944. The German Nazi army was sent to Slovakia quite promptly by the Nazi government as a "friendly help" to the Slovakian Nazi government, of course on their request. Militarily, the uprising was supported by battalions of the Slovak army, which changed its allegiance from the Slovak Nazi government to the Czech government in exile. However, the Slovak battalions were no match for the German army, and the uprising was brutally crushed. A key German unit was the SS Edelweiss Division, famous for its experience in dealing with civilian uprising sympathizers. The extent of their atrocities was probably never fully discovered, as mass graves and burned out villages kept appearing in the mountain region of Slovakia for several years after the war.

Although the uprising lasted for no more than two months, it had a significant effect. It kept several divisions of the Nazi army well-occupied, thus lessening the Nazi pressure on the Eastern Front. This helped the Red Army and the Allies in their spring 1945 offensive over the Carpathian Mountains.

The end of the uprising was also the time when Rasti moved with the partisans to the Tatra Mountains to hide. He changed his identity again, this time to George Rastislav Lenda. It was not an easy time for them. The contingent of the Nazi army left behind had a mop-up task. They started to hunt the partisans, and pushed them high into the mountains where essential supplies were limited. There was however plenty of snow, so the hiding was good as long as they would not make their presence obvious with chimney smoke, or shooting at the Nazi patrols. Of course the left-behind Nazi patrols were not too enthusiastic about getting into shooting battles with the partisans either. After all, the partisans could hide well, and could shoot at the patrols without being seen. So the main fighting strategy of the Nazi army was to plant personnel mine fields everywhere when they suspected the partisan's presence. The partisan's strategy was to watch the Nazi army installing the mine fields, and dismantle them after the Nazi patrols left. Of course there were some accidents, and this kept Rasti quite busy practicing his medical profession.

The partisans were under strict orders not to shoot at the patrols, as this would betray their own presence. It might result in a temporary victory, but it would trigger a counterattack by a much stronger force. Finally, it would result in evacuation of their hiding place and a move to more distant locations, further from their supply lines.

However, there were occasions when the opportunity to kill the enemy with a single shot was too tempting. A newly recruited partisan would shoot at the Nazi patrol and the patrol counterattacked, wounding the partisan. Then the Nazi patrol returned to its base. Rasti was there and would provide first aid to the wounded partisan, then carry him to safety higher in the mountains. It took some time and effort, and during one of these rescues Rasti's own right leg froze. When at last they made it back to the hut, Rasti had saved his comrade and his own leg as well. But the leg was never good again. Trouble with this leg came back occasionally, and much later a thrombosis in his right leg would be the ultimate cause of Rasti's death.

In the Czech Army

My Uncle Fred joined the Czechoslovakian Army when the Red Army and the Allied Czechoslovakian Army crossed over the Carpathian Mountains into Slovakia in the spring of 1945. He had been a reserve officer in the prewar Czechoslovakian Army, and now he became a military physician with the rank of captain in the new Czech Army. As such, he participated in the liberation fights on the Eastern Front.

Again, treacherous land mines kept him busy. There were many occasions when he had to take care of soldiers wounded badly by enemy mines and enemy fire. There were also occasions when he had to help soldiers wounded by friendly fire, or accidents with their own weapons.

Early one morning Rasti was ordered to jump into a military jeep and travel as fast as possible to a unit on the front lines where some of these self-inflicted accidents had happened during personal gun cleaning procedures. He arrived safely and took care of the wounds. However, another vehicle which followed his jeep tracks later in the day was blown to pieces by an exploding mine. Apparently the ground was still frozen when Rasti drove over it in his jeep early in the morning, or it was just luck.

Rasti's brother Paul, my father, had joined the Czechoslovakian Army after he escaped from the Auschwitz Death March. However, the two brothers did not know of each other's whereabouts. They had last seen each other years before at the railway station in Prague, when Paul and his family were about to be Transported to the Terezin concentration camp.

As Rasti had changed his name from Fred Lustig to various other names when he was active in the underground resistance, with the partisans and with the army, there was no chance that his brother Paul could find him. Rasti knew that most of the men from Terezin were transported to extermination camps in Poland where they were killed routinely in gas chambers, or died as a result of disease, starvation, or work accidents. Or were shot by guards for no reason at all. However, Rasti was determined to try to locate his older brother. He assumed that, had his brother survived, he might have had the same motivation as he to use the opportunity to fight back at the Nazis by joining the Red Army. With some effort and luck, Rasti discovered that his older brother was, in fact, a soldier in the same army as he was.

Although he knew the chance of finding Paul was slim, he asked his soldier clerk to help him to search the Czechoslovakian Army recruits records. After extensive searching, they got lucky and found the old family name in the volunteers' listings. After that, finding his brother's unit was not too easy, either, as the army was on constant and rapid move all the time. Rasti succeeded in this as well with his typical perseverance.

Is This You, Fred?

And so it happened that, on one rainy evening early in the spring of 1945, an army jeep drove up to a certain little village house close to the front lines, and unexpectedly stopped. A Czechoslovakian Army medical captain jumped out of the jeep and entered the house. After asking the owner where the sleeping quarters of the soldiers were, he entered a dimly lit back room. The four Czechoslovakian soldiers inside were caught by absolute surprise.

The four soldiers, all of them of Jewish origin, were sick with colds, taking turns coughing and sneezing. They were not shaved too well, and their uniforms were far from being in perfect shape, mostly wrinkled and not too clean. In addition, they had added some civilian scarves for warmth, which was definitely in conflict with regulations. The soldiers were busy trying to get some heat out of the little stove in the back of the room, their backs to the doorway. The stove persistently resisted. It only smoked, and did not heat. The whole room was full of smoke, so they opened the one small window they had, which in turn made the room cold again. In general, the soldiers were miserable, and naturally not in the best mood.

A surprise visit by an officer was not really welcomed at all, not even a visit by a medical officer.

The soldiers did not expect a physician's visit. Although they were sick, their sickness did not warrant a medical officer's visit. So they were surprised when the officer entered the smoky, dark room that evening.

By regulation the first soldier seeing an officer enter a room was supposed to call all the soldiers to attention, and then report to the officer the status of the unit. So after a few moments of silence it happened to be Paul who coughed out the word "to attention" and started to report that four soldiers of the transportation unit were in place. The captain barked the regular "at ease" as he was used to doing automatically, and started to look around.

At that time Paul became somewhat suspicious, and coughed out,

"Is this you, Fred?"

Which was, of course completely against all regulations, and a serious breach of discipline. To the surprise of the other three soldiers present, a very friendly hugging followed, and some wetness of eyes was also noticeable.

First they asked each other about the whereabouts of their father, and sadly concluded that he mostly likely had not survived. By this time, both of them were familiar enough with the circumstances of the war, and the sad reality of the fate Paul had seen in Auschwitz daily: hundreds of mothers with children walking from the transport trains directly to the gas chambers, thinking they were going to take a shower.

Rasti told Paul that he heard his fiancée Bela was all right in Prague some time ago. However, there was always a risk of unfortunate happenings, as she was affiliated with the Czech underground resistance, and the

Gestapo were still very active in Prague. Their third brother, Otto, the youngest one, presumably went to China by ship at the beginning of the war, and nobody had heard about him since.

Rasti told Paul about the change of his name, and he added that his intention was to keep the new last name in the future. Paul agreed that this might be a good idea for him as well, and he would take the needed steps to make it official.

Just before leaving, Rasti asked Paul if there was anything he might need right now. Paul said that he actually had all he needed. After all, the army took care of him quite well under the given circumstances of war conditions. He definitely was not spoiled after living in Nazi concentration camps for three years. However, when Rasti insisted, Paul said he only had one additional thing he would like to have: a violin. He was a skilled musician, and he missed the music. Before departing, Rasti, as an experienced partisan, also gave the four soldiers in the small room some beneficial suggestions about how to make a fire with damp wood, and not the best chimney draft.

A not too new, but nice violin was delivered to Paul sometime later. It was not only for his benefit. The violin and the musician with it soon became a very popular pair with the rest of the soldiers in the unit. They served well for the betterment of the soldiers' morale in the difficult days that followed.

The brothers kept in touch for the rest of the war, and met occasionally. Although both of them experienced some close encounters during the rest of the war, they both survived. For their activity, they both were awarded medals. Paul received a Medal of Valor. It was an extraordinary achievement, considering the short period of time he was with the army. He joined the army sometime in February 1945, and the war ended for him in April of the same year.

Rasti was awarded the highest Czechoslovakian medal of all, the Medal of the White Lion. This was in recognition of his extraordinary valor and personal courage during the war fighting against Nazi Germany. However, it was mostly in recognition of his contribution to the effort to reestablish a free Czechoslovakia again after the end of the war.

Rasti returned to Prague with the Czechoslovakian Army in 1945 and married Bela shortly afterwards. He returned to civilian life after being promoted to the rank of major, and being demobilized. He reestablished his prewar physician's practice in Prague. However, this venture was disrupted shortly afterwards as the process of communist nationalization engulfed the medical profession, as well as all the rest of private enterprise. The rest of his life was peppered with frustrations, mostly resulting from the communist takeover of Czechoslovakia in 1948. The most frustrating for him was the communist effort to rewrite history, and to portray the Slovakian national fight for freedom during the war as being managed and carried out by the Communist Party.

Paul was demobilized with the rank of first lieutenant, and became the director of a textile factory, and later the business director of Moravolen, a textile conglomerate in northern Moravia. As such, he traveled to western Europe and to America. However, his manufacturing career came to an end shortly after the communist takeover in Czechoslovakia. His last employment before retirement was with the local highway department. Occasionally, he still played his violin for the amusement of his family and friends.

~~~

Chapter Seven
The End of the War

The Transports Increase

It is said that it was actually Rabbi Judah Loew ben Bezalel, creator of the *Golem* legend, who discovered the Theory of Relativity in Prague a long time ago, at the end of the sixteenth century. This is the story about it:

A poor man goes to the, rabbi and complains, "My house is much too small for my family of ten."

"Bring your goat into the house," says the rabbi, and the man complies. A week later he returns.

"Rabbi, it's even worse!"

"Bring your chickens into the house," says the rabbi.

The man returns in another week, still complaining, and the rabbi tells him to bring in his cow as well. The next time the man comes, he is at his wits' end.

"I can't stand it any longer," he says.

"In that case," says the rabbi, "go home and take all your animals back out to the barn."

"Thank you, Rabbi," the man says a few days later, "We have so much room now!"

The Nazis came up with a lot of ways to cover up their war crimes. One of the ways was to show Terezin as a recreational facility where the Jews lived in a comfortable environment: "At the same time the Aryan German Super-People had to suffer while trying to save the civilization." The Allied armies were crushing the Thousand Year Nazi Paradise now, and the Nazis did not like it one bit.

It was sometime around then that we kids moved into our third Heim. It had been a school building, originally. It was located on the outskirts of the permitted area, and across from it was a concrete wall beyond which we could see, from our windows, a modern concrete barracks building occupied by Nazi military personnel.

Terezin was emptied to turn it into a so-called recreational facility, a "City Given to the Jews by Hitler." That was the planned title of a propaganda film. Luckily for the inventors of the film idea, Hitler never knew about it. In any event the film, although almost completed sometime in March of 1945, was never distributed to the public cinemas. Only fragments of it were found after the war. To make the film, Terezin's over-populated status had to be reduced to a normal environment. The solution was, of course, to vacate the concentration camp by sending the prisoners to the extermination camps in the East. And this also brought them closer to their "Final Solution" of the Jewish Problem, extinguishing the entire Jewish race.

As the transports progressed in the fall of 1944 the ghetto became less crowded. Suddenly, there was plenty of space. No longer was one closely surrounded by many other people on the street. Now, one could walk or run without being bumped by others. But there was a strange feeling that someone was missing. And it was not only one missing in every family, for mostly whole families were missing, and sometimes there was no one left to miss them, for their friends were gone as well. There was no end to the transports in sight; at least not for the commoners. However, the prominent people were no longer comfortable either. Practically all of the prisoners were living under a constant threat, never knowing when their time would come. The rules of selection could only be imagined, and rumors were taken very seriously.

My Adopted Brother

I have already mentioned my "adopted" brother. At one time children without parents in Terezin were the prime target for transports to the East. Obviously Rudi, the child my parents had unofficially adopted just before we went to Terezin, was one of them. In addition to not having his legal parents with him, Rudi was also not in the best of health. As a result, he was living in a special Heim for sick children. Then his time came, and he was selected for transport. In the case of children, this always meant a transport to the death chamber. This was not known for certain in Terezin, but the general feeling was that "transport" meant a trip of no return. This applied especially to those who were not in good health. They had almost no chance of surviving, even though the end of the war was so close.

My mother learned that Rudi had been selected for transport, and she started a furious effort to save him. As a qualified nurse in the general hospital, she was one of those who were considered indispensable. She started an effort generally considered impossible: to have a child removed from a transport list. She talked to the transport people and to all kinds of officials to convince them that Rudi was not actually a child without parents, thus not at all in line for transport to the East. This did not bring too many results, so she took a gamble and announced that she would volunteer as a nurse and go with Rudi, and of course with me as well. It was obviously not a rational solution, but it was an honest approach in consideration of the promise she had made when she took Rudi under our family umbrella. Next, she made it quite clear in the hospital that she was ready to go through with her plan.

And she was serious. Finally the hospital people, mostly respected doctors, got involved and put their weight behind their statement that Irene was indeed an indispensable member of the hospital staff and that she should be the last person to be transported, if at all. Nevertheless, it took a lot of additional effort to convince the officials that Rudi's name should be removed from the list. The decision was made at almost the last minute, but Rudi stayed and survived. Of course, most likely someone else had to go instead of him.

Red Cross Inspections

In conjunction with efficiently vacating the concentration camp, the Nazis organized a Swiss Red Cross inspection in the summer of 1944. Gradually, some improvements were made in the general appearance of the concentration camp itself. The general beautification effort was noticeable. Fancy new wooden signs pointing in different directions appeared, probably like in a

German spa town. There were wooden benches installed, and several parks with flowerbeds appeared. Some buildings received a new coat of paint. Signs indicating "restaurants" and other "shops" were displayed. Sidewalks were washed, and everything visible was cleaned. The preparation for a big show was in the air.

When everything was ready, the inspection by the International Red Cross was arranged. The inspection was made in a carefully prearranged fashion, like a well-planned performance. For example, the inspectors were taken to a newly established kindergarten, and the children were given bread with sardines just before the inspectors arrived, guided by the camp commander, Mr. Rahm. As instructed, the children turned to the commander and said in German, *"Sardines again, Uncle Rahm?"* This was to demonstrate how well the children were being treated, and how spoiled they were at a time when most of the children in countries under Nazi management were starving. Similar performances in other locations along the preplanned route took place. For example, selected children were given good food for several weeks. These children had to parade in front of the inspectors to prove how well-fed the children in Terezin were. For me, this was the first time I was taken to a "restaurant" with the other kids of our Heim, and we ate ice cream. All in all, the inspectors were satisfied, and the SS management was satisfied as well.

The Nazis were encouraged with the success of their beautification show, and did not want to waste the effort. So they came up with their propaganda film idea. Some theater and concert performances had already been prepared for the big inspection show, so they were included in the propaganda film as cultural performances were believed by the Nazis to be a typical part of the Jewish lifestyle. (Although Joseph Goebbels, the Nazi Culture and Propaganda Minister, was known for saying, "I reach for my revolver whenever I hear the word *culture.*") He had obviously not been involved in the production of "Hitler Gave a Town to the Jews."

The Nazi propaganda film also included the now famous children's opera, "Brundibar," revived and performed in Terezin. This opera was normally performed in an attic of one of the old barracks. However, with this Nazi show preparation and the making of the propaganda film, the "Brundibar" performance was moved to a real stage in another building, a building located outside the normal ghetto boundaries. This building was made accessible to Jews, but only for this special occasion.

Some of us in our Heim were selected to participate as "audience members." We were given new white shirts and taken to this nice, clean building that had a decent auditorium with balconies. We were instructed not to look back, but only to the stage in front of us. Naturally, I peeked back several times. There were SS officers in the balconies manning reflectors pointed at the stage and at us, to provide enough light for filming. We could tell the performance was not done fully, and that several scenes were repeated, so it was not very good in terms of entertainment. In any event, we all knew the whole opera well by now, and most of us could probably sing along, if permitted. At any rate we made it through unharmed; it used to be a Nazi practice to enroll all performers and participants in the next available transport, but this time was an exception. We survived, and were allowed to keep the white shirts as well.

Replenishing the Stock

Apparently the Nazis did not feel too comfortable with the "empty" concentration camp. Or perhaps they were making a stronger effort to find every last Jew who was still free. So they decided to scrape the bottom of the barrel, as there were not too many Jews left outside of Terezin. There were some mixed marriages, and they were forced to divorce. The Jewish members of those marriages, until then protected by marriage to non-Jews, were now sent to Terezin.

We had some newcomers in our Heim as well. One day a tall boy appeared as a new addition. He spoke only German, however we could communicate with him reasonably by that time, mostly thanks to our additional German supervisor. It turned out the boy was somewhat older than most of us, and had come directly from Berlin with his mother. He was still fully brainwashed with Nazi propaganda. He would tell us about his father, who was apparently not Jewish, but had married a Jewish woman. His father was a firefighter. The boy would talk about his father enthusiastically, telling us how physically capable he was. He could run several blocks without stopping, lift a lot of heavy things, and was never afraid of fire at all.

The boy had brought with him a German encyclopedia, and he would often show it to us. He proudly found Hitler's picture in the book, and explained to us that this was the Leader (*Führer*) and explained how smart and good looking the Führer was. At that point Hanka, our supervisor in charge and teacher, appeared and closed the book quite angrily. She told this boy bluntly that his Führer was personally responsible for most of the horrors of the war, and specifically for the deaths of most of our Jewish friends who had vanished in the transports and were never heard of again. Presumably they were not alive any more. She told the boy that he should not be so proud of his father, either. This man who married his mother did not stick by her, and divorced her to save his own skin. By letting his wife, and his son, go to Terezin he exposed them to the possibility (probability) of being enlisted in a transport to the place of no return, to the East. Sure enough, the boy did not stay with us too long.

There was also a very little boy called Peterko, which is a term of endearment for Peter in the Slovak language. We were told that he was only three years old, a tiny little boy who came from Slovakia. He was instantly beloved by the whole Heim. Everybody felt sorry for him, and wanted to take care of him. Apparently he had no parents in Terezin at all. He disappeared soon, and lived in our memories only.

One of my Uncles arrived one day as well. His wife, who was not Jewish, had stuck by him as long as possible, but finally gave up in order to save their daughter's life. He was my Uncle Franta's older brother, Pepik (a nickname for Joseph.) Franta was also still in Terezin, but he could not go to meet his brother. So my mother was asked to go to the *Šlojska* (the place where new arrivals were kept) and to take care of Pepik. She put on her white nurse's uniform, and with some effort penetrated the guarded access to the new arrivals. Pepik was very distressed; the circumstances for the new arrivals in the Šlojska were very depressing. My mother asked Pepik if he was hungry, and he said he was. She reached into her pocket, and gave him a roll. This was like a life-saving act to Pepik, and he never forgot it. He made it through the war, and never forgot this small good deed. (After the war Pepik became a director of the coal distribution office in Communist Czechoslovakia. We always had enough coal in the winter thanks to Pepik, even though he lived in Prague and we lived in a small town in northern Moravia.)

The Beginning of the End

Towards the end of the war we saw lots of small airplanes flying high in the sky almost daily. The airplanes had little steam tails behind them (although they were not jets) and they were dropping aluminum foil strips to confuse the Nazi radars. Sometimes sirens sounded an alarm. Nobody took it seriously enough to run for cover. In any event, we did not have any shelters to run to.

Our Heim at that time was located at the outskirts of Terezin. Across the wall was a Nazi soldiers' compound with a relatively modern barracks, separated from the Terezin concentration camp by a high concrete wall. However, we could see into some parts of the compound from our windows on the third floor. Sometimes we could see the fanatical Nazi soldiers shooting from their roof at the small bombers flying high in the sky. Hanka would come and tell us to get away from the windows because there was an air raid alarm in force. However she would also say, "Look at the Nazi soldier fools, they must be really desperate. Their end must be pretty close." And it was.

One night we saw some unusual lights in the sky to the north and we did not know what it could be. Later the rumor spread that the Allies had bombarded the whole city of Dresden (about 90 kilometers to the north) out of existence, as there were some biological laboratories where the Nazis were developing deadly disease viruses. And nobody was sorry for those people over there that were losing their property and lives. After all, they were our enemies and they were killing us without mercy.

A Death March Reaches Terezin

Towards the end of the war there was something new for us to see almost every day. However, one of the events impressed forever on my mind was an encounter with a death march. It was one of those "Come and look!" events. As usual, the word would spread around, and then somebody would say we should go and see.

It was at the main incoming road from outside the ghetto, right on the street along the main square near the SS Commandature. There was a wall of onlookers: Terezin prisoners of all ages. They were mostly silent, just standing and watching. It was a scene hard to believe and hard to forget. A group of about fifty people, dressed in dirty uniforms with blue and white horizontal stripes, were drifting slowly along the street. Some of them were falling down as they went. There was a cordon of Terezin prisoners holding hands and walking alongside the drifting people to separate them from the onlookers. The fallen people were picked up by other Terezin prisoners, placed on stretchers, and carried away. Suddenly one of the onlookers threw a little piece of Terezin cake, a pound cake, into the midst of the drifting people. Those who were close to the fallen piece of yellow cake grabbed it from the road, and those who did not get it tried to take it away from them. It was like a chicken fight at feeding time. They had forgotten any sense of human dignity, or any other feelings, long before. All that remained was a living creature's sense of survival. But most of the people kept on drifting along, with the apathy of drifters who just keep doing what they had been doing a little while ago. It was the only thing they could do without thinking about their next move. Just drifting along, pushed by an effort to survive.

We were told these poor people were mostly Polish Jews from concentration camps in the East, survivors like us, but in much worse shape. They were placed into isolated housing, quarantine, because they were sick, mostly with typhus. Should we see them on the street, we should avoid contact with them. Indeed, several days later we met some of them who seemed to be more industrious than the others. Apparently they had broken out of the quarantine and started to walk the streets, wearing the civilian clothes they had been given in place of the dirty stripped prison uniforms. They would approach us and ask for food, mostly in Polish, with some German and fragments of Czech. We did not avoid them, because we were very curious as to who those people were. However, our intention to communicate with them was always interrupted by some local adults. Mostly they would tell those people that they should be ashamed to do that, as they were spreading their disease to the last few surviving children of Terezin. (In fact, the typhus spread anyway. Terezin was isolated from the rest of the outside world when the war ended. Nobody was allowed to leave the camp.)

It was probably at that time that my mother made a promise to God. She would not leave the hospital, even if she could, and would stay and take care of the patients, if only my father returned to us safely after the war.

The Liberation of Terezin

The weather was nice again, a sunny and warm spring day. There was an uprising in Prague and it echoed in Terezin. There were some dramatic happenings in the ghetto, but we in the Heim heard rumors only, and we did not understand them anyway.

When the liberators came, we saw them only occasionally and at a distance, as we were still trapped behind the fence. Now we were being guarded by Czechoslovakian police. Terezin was still locked up because of the outbreak of typhus. We were allowed to peek through the partially opened gate where the old wooden fence was, as erected by the Nazi management of the ghetto so they would not have to mix with Jews. I approached the slightly opened gate to peek out to see the world. There was a Czechoslovakian policeman guarding the gate. He gave me a little piece of chocolate, probably to compensate me for not letting me out. I did not really know how to thank him. Was he still speaking German as the previous guards did? Maybe they just changed some patches on their uniforms but were still the same people. Or maybe he was not afraid to speak the Czech language now that the Nazis were gone. So I decided to risk it, and thanked him in Czech, *"Děkuji."* It worked! He let me peek through the partly opened gate to see the free world. For a little while I was allowed to see far off into open space. Then he closed the gate, probably so our typhus bugs would not spread out into his freshly liberated world. Well, the piece of chocolate he gave me tasted good anyway, and I ran off.

The closure eased little by little with time. We were standing at the unguarded open gate in the old city fortification. It was where my father used to have his "private office" before he disappeared in a transport to the East. The open gate went through the old fortification. There was the main road outside and, further along another fortification, the Small Fortress, which had been the SS prison. There was quite a lot of traffic on the road along the river.

The Red Army

Suddenly we saw the Red Army Cavalry through the gate where my father used to have a "Private Transportleitung Office." The cavalry was passing by on the road alongside the ghetto, and we did not know from where or where to. There must have been hundreds of carts pulled by pairs of horses, one after another, running very fast. It was an impressive show in the days of armored vehicles, tanks, and all the other mechanization the Nazis occasionally demonstrated. We had not seen live animals, especially horses, for years, if ever.

We saw large military vehicles full of soldiers, parked in the yard of the hospital compound where my mother lived and worked. The soldiers were friendly, and invited us to climb into the vehicle cabins and sit behind the steering wheels, just to try it out. They spoke Russian, so we hardly understood them. Sign language was the effective means of communication.

The soldiers inside the hospital were wounded badly. The fight for our freedom was not just glory for them, and we had the most appreciative feelings toward them. Those soldiers were our real heroes. Some of them had limbs amputated, and most of them were in great pain. Some of them kept their revolvers under their pillows. They did not want to be moved, even to have their bed made, because any movement of their bodies was very painful for them. They did not want to be moved at all. One of them even pointed his revolver at my mother when she insisted on making his bed, so she left him alone.

Erna and Hanka at the end of the War

Life at our Heim proceeded as closely to our normal routines as possible. However some changes were noticeable even to us. One of them was that Erna, our second supervisor, manufactured a little red star with a hammer and sickle painted on it, and had it displayed quite prominently on her blouse. So she was expressing her appreciation of the Red Army effort and sacrifices. Hanka had a Czechoslovakian tricolor attached. Being in charge, she felt she should continue her educational duties as well. We had a regular class meeting, and Hanka explained to us the situation as she saw it. She appreciated the sacrifices of the Red Army soldiers, but at the same time she explained that the freedom we had gained from the Soviet Union effort might turn out differently pretty soon. In a certain light, there was not too much difference between Russian power and German power. She explained that the Soviet Union was not actually a free democratic country, and there were concentration camps there as well. In addition, historically the Russians were not the greatest friends of Jews, and they were treating their own Jewish population accordingly.

Interestingly enough, sometime after the war Erna embraced the capitalist world and married a wealthy person in Great Britain, as Hanka told me when we would meet occasionally. On the other hand, Hanka embraced the communist regime quite successfully. Later on, she became a headmaster, and finally a school district manager. She also married a high-ranking member of the Communist Party Politburo, with all the privileges attached.

None of this could diminish my appreciation for those two ladies at all. They indeed risked their lives to provide a high quality of education for us, which had been strictly forbidden. They were aware that, if the Nazis caught them, at the very least they would have been selected for the first transportation opportunity to the East, with no return ticket. They could have been arrested and sentenced directly to torture and death in the attached Small Fortress across the river for intentionally disobeying rules.

I met Hanka again when I visited Czechoslovakia after the communist regime collapsed. She was a widow at the time, but still a devoted communist. Although retired. she was teaching dialectical materialism theory at the Communist Party school. At that time she expressed concern that the Communist Party in the new Czechoslovakia might be declared an illegal organization. I assured her that this was very unlikely to happen in the new Czechoslovakia, arguing that the current model of democracy, the USA, permitted a Communist Party to exist quite legally.

The Best Birthday Present

My ninth birthday was on 25 May, and it was a nice day again. I was in the Heim (our "Home") in the morning as usual, when a nurse friend of my mother came and told Hanka that I should go with her to my mother's quarters. She would not say too much to me, just that my mother had prepared a birthday celebration for me, so I should hurry over with her. Of course I suspected something since a normal celebration, if any, would come in the afternoon, when I would go to visit my mother by myself.

There, on my mother's bunk bed, sat my father in a military uniform as a birthday gift for me! It was the best gift for my birthday I could ever dream of!

We hugged and kissed, and talked. My father insisted we leave at once, and arrangements were made to leave. We were in a hurry to catch the train to Prague. I was not allowed to return to the Heim to say goodbye to

Hanka, Erna, and my friends. My mother's nurse friend volunteered to go to the Heim with a small suitcase, to fill it with my few belongings and to say goodbye to everyone on my behalf. We were on our way as soon as she made it back.

The Terezin Concentration Camp's exits were still guarded, this time by Russian soldiers. We were not supposed to leave, because of the typhoid quarantine, and I asked my father what we would do if we were stopped. He just patted his revolver at his belt and said that nobody would try to top us. We walked right by the guard, and he didn't say a thing, he just saluted my father. My father returned the salute and off we went, free at last.

We traveled by train to Prague and stayed with my Uncle for several days. My mother then returned to Terezin to fulfill her promise to God. The typhoid quarantine was over in about a month, and the Terezin Concentration Camp was finally emptied, and closed.

~~~

Chapter Eight
After the War

Our Family Finally Reunited

While my mother was still nursing the sick in Terezin, I traveled with my father to Hranečnik, his duty place. It was located in northern Moravia, close to the industrial city of Ostrava. The train was full of soldiers, and my father handed me through the window and then got in through the door with some effort himself. It was all new to me, but I handled it well. My father proudly tested me on the subject of Czech history and other items to demonstrate that I had some education, although I had been behind the concentration camp walls for three years, and was not supposed to learn anything at all.

We arrived at my father's military unit, and he found accommodations for me with a family in a little house close to his barracks. He enrolled me also in the local school, since it was not the end of the school year yet. Surprisingly, I could start the school at the same level with children of my age, although it was the first time I attended an ordinary, official school.

About a month later when the typhoid epidemic in Terezin ended and my mother finished her nursing duty there and Terezin was finally closed, she went to Radesovice, where we had lived before the war. The authorities gave her an apartment in a villa next to the one we used to live in. The Jewish friends of ours who had lived there at the same time as we did were gone forever. They had been replaced by a German military family, who then left at the end of the war. My mother cleaned the apartment, and prepared for my father and I to arrive.

In the meantime, however, we were invited to live on a farm owned by my aunt's family. She had been the wife of my mother's brother, Leo, whom she had divorced at the beginning of the Nazi occupation. He had volunteered to go to Terezin with his mother, my grandma. They were both already gone when we arrived in Terezin, and we never saw them again. They were murdered in one of the concentration camps in the East.

My father brought me back when the school year ended. My mom and I began living on the farm so we could gain some weight. There was still a shortage of food, so rationing of food was still in effect. Life on the farm had some advantages in that respect. Occasionally, we visited the apartment in Radesovice that my mom had prepared for us. Our good friends gave us back the valuables they had hidden for us, mostly family photos and 8mm films. We expected that my father would join us as soon as he was demobilized, and we would start our life again where we had ended it before the war. We did not know then how differently things would turn out.

The Macholds Family

My father was finally demobilized a few months later. He was offered a textile manager's position in Bruntal (Freundentahl in German) and he accepted the position. So we moved to Bruntal, west of Ostrava, near the Jeseniky Mountains.

This was in the northern part of prewar Czechoslovakia, in the territory called "Sudetenland" by the Germans. It was the part of Czechoslovakia where the population was mostly German. The German population had voted in a referendum in 1938 to become associated with Nazi Germany, and they were. Now, after the war, this territory had become part of Czechoslovakia again. The German property was "nationalized" (confiscated) by the new Czechoslovak government, and the Germans were sent to Germany.

The textile factory where my father was given the Manager's position was also confiscated German property. It used to belong to a family of three brothers, the Macholds. Next to the factory were three nice villas, the residences of the owners, and we were entitled to occupy one of them. Another one was occupied by my father's assistant, Mr. Friedner. He was also a demobilized Jewish soldier, and my father's friend. The third villa was occupied by the local representative to the new Congress of the Czechoslovak Republic.

There had also been a concentration camp adjacent to the textile factory and the villas property. The factory used to produce fine linen and table cloths for export before the war. However, during the war they produced military uniforms and gas masks. A slave labor concentration camp had been attached to the factory. There prisoners, mostly Jews, supplemented the regular German laborers. The Macholds had treated the prisoners well. They supplemented their food, and treated the prisoners humanely. However, the SS guards were ordered to organize a Death March with the prisoners at the end of the war, when the Red Army was approaching. This was bad news. It was known that the prisoners were not fed during these marches, and were treated badly. The guards were ordered to shoot those who were not able to continue, when they collapsed.

The Macholds argued with the SS commander to leave the prisoners in the concentration camp, and to disappear and save their own skin. It was a risky proposition. In fact, the Macholds were telling the SS commander to disobey orders, and they were encouraging the guards to desert. It was know that there was an SS unit specifically organized to find deserters, and shoot them on the spot. The Macholds risked their own lives, also; they could have been shot as well. Luckily they prevailed, and lots of prisoners' lives were saved.

The situation changed dramatically after the liberation. The prisoners were freed from the concentration camp as soon as the Red Army took over, and the German population was suddenly not on the winning side. They were all to be deported to Germany. In the meantime, all the local German population from nearby houses was put into the concentration camp where the Jewish prisoners used to be. They continued working in the factory, as they used to, it was just their housing conditions that had changed. Their nice houses were confiscated, and given to the Czech and Slovak population which was encouraged to move into what had been the Sudetenland territory.

The Macholds were placed in the concentration camp also. However, when my father took over the management of the factory, he was told about the heroic behavior of the Macholds during the war: specifically, how they saved the prisoners from the Death March. My father knew well the conditions of the Death March, because he himself had experienced one just before he had escaped from the Nazis. So he arranged that the Macholds could move out of the concentration camp, into the villa with us. They moved into the basement apartment where the housekeeper used to live. In addition, they were allowed to use the attic space originally designated as guest bedrooms.

The Macholds were actually a large family. There were three brothers. However, I remember the eldest one who lived with us. They had four children; three of them were there when we arrived. The youngest one was a boy, named Dietrich; he was one year older than me. Dietrich had a sister one year older than him, and a brother who was two years older who was about 13 at the time. They also had a grandfather living with them.

There was a farm associated with the textile factory. It was located several hundred yards down the street from where we lived. The older Machold brother apparently was interested in agriculture, so he worked on the farm. He also did some gardening in the large gardens around the villa we lived in, and still had feelings of ownership towards the property. He would tell me off when he saw I accidentally nicked some wall, or treated the property without respect. He apparently believed that the Macholds would get the property back one day. We could sympathize with those feelings; we went through the same feelings several years before, when the Nazis took over Czechoslovakia and confiscated Jewish properties.

There were several shallow bunkers in the garden, and we were told that they had been built to satisfy some Nazi regulation about personnel protection in case of an air raid. So we left them as they were for the time being. However, a German worker in the textile factory misspoke one day, and it came out that the walls of the bunkers were full of the Machold's precious porcelain. It was a disappointment for them when it all became the property of the Czechoslovak State, for sale to all its citizens, including us.

In general we had a friendly relationship with the Macholds, and we believed they had a friendly attitude toward us as well. But it had its limits. It turned out that there was another member of the family, the eldest brother of Dietrich. The eldest brother appeared at the villa one day, and the Macholds proudly introduced him to my father. It came out that he used to be an SS officer, and he was just released from a prisoner of war camp. My father spoke with him shortly, but he refused to shake his hand.

Finally, after several months in the concentration camp, the German population in Bruntal was sent to Germany. They were allowed to take 75 kilograms of belongings, a little more than we had been allowed when we went to Terezin. A truck showed up one day at the villa where the Macholds lived with us, and they loaded the truck with their belongings. They were allowed to move to Austria, and then to Lichtenstein. Presumably they had some assets deposited safely there. Maybe the

Macholds will be recognized one day as those who saved so many Jews, the Righteous Among the Nations.

~~~

My Father's Letter to Relatives in the USA
(Tanslated from German by Ms. Modessa Jacobs)

in Bruntal,
Vrchlickeho Str. 8
10 September 1945

My loved ones all together!

I am using this first opportunity to write to you all and thank you profusely from my heart for your telegram, and the $100 you transferred to us. However, we have not kept it for ourselves. We left the money in the care of Marile Klopfer, and would like to use it for Otto and Leo, who surely have an essential need for it.

Now that we have survived this horrible war, you all don't need to worry about us anymore. We are some of the very few exceptions who through chance, luck, and all possible lucky circumstances were saved and have already begun a totally normal life.

There are no words to tell you how much Marile Klopfer helped us with her packets, because they came during the worst time, when all of Theresienstadt (Terezin) was starving, and we were often dependent upon her help alone. That we naturally can never forget her, you will all understand.

I have taken over the management of the textile factory Machold Bruntal, and I am fully absorbed in this work. We are living fairly well, and do not suffer any hunger. Naturally we miss the most our loved ones who perished in the various concentration camps in Poland.

Tommy has been going to school since a few days ago. He has not had much instruction yet, but we are hoping that he will come along well in school, since the Czechoslovakian children were not allowed to learn much during the German occupation. Irene is busy with household chores and is getting the home in order.

Fred wrote to us just yesterday that he is being demobilized and is beginning his private practice again. He got married after a fifteen year acquaintance, and spent his honeymoon in Karlsbad with his wife, Mrs. Bela, *born as* Dolezalova (gynecologist) and is beginning his normal life. You all already know that he fled to Slovakia in 1942, where he hid in the Slovakian mountains under other names, then enlisted in the Czechoslovakian Army and luckily returned home with the rank of a captain. At the moment he is still serving in the Army Ministry.

In three days, 12 September, it will be exactly three years ago that we were deported to Theresienstadt. Unfortunately, we met neither my father nor the Getreuers or Anspachs, or the Munich Ableses either. They were already further transported to Poland, and probably perished there. We were only together with Aunt Martha and Liesl until 1944. Uncle Epstein could stay in Prague, because he was engaged in an economically important production. Aunt and Liesl could stay in Theresienstadt because of the so-called family disruption rule. But after Uncle Ernst came to Theresienstadt, all three of them went to Poland. Uncle Ernst was a patient of my wife at the Hospital. Aunt Martha worked as a wash woman in the central laundry, and Liesl worked as a dress maker in a sewing factory.

They were often hungry. We know from Trude Anspach, that she worked in agriculture as a sheep hereder, and that she went to Poland with her parents willingly. The old Abeles left for Poland with the so-called eldertransport to Poland several days before we arrived. We only met Gretl Abeles in Theresienstadt; she was working as a cleaning lady at the hospital. From my father's side, Uncle Rudolf and Aunt Gusti died in Theresienstadt, Uncle Ignaz and his son Josef went further into Poland, and did not come back. My wife lost her mother, both her brothers, as well as all her father's sisters.

In Pilsen, out of 4,500 Jews, barely 100 came back; in Bohemia and Moravia out of 110,000 barely 7,000. In Auschwitz, in principle all mothers with children up to 14 years, and all people over 50 years, were gassed, so that there are barely 50 Jewish children with us. I was able to sustain myself in Auschwitz as a worker, and in the last moment I was freed by the Russians. My wife and Tommy were sustained only because of my wife's unique qualifications. She was one of the typhus and TBC station nurses during the worst epidemic.

We lost nearly all our apartment furnishings, jewelry, clothes, and linen. But we don't miss them all that much. From the state we have already received a lot of replacements, and with time we will be able to procure the rest. In any case, we have the most important things, and you all do not need to worry about us anymore. We are not hungry and, except for small things, one does not even notice that three months ago there was a war here. We have invited Uncle Moritz and Aunt Anette to come to us, so that Mariele can travel to her life in America. They will be in the best hands with us.

Rudl Werner and Ernst Lewvy also came back with the Czechoslovakian Army. They were both in Palestine. Ernst has family there. Marile wrote us that the sons of Fritz Klauber are in the American Army in Europe. Maybe you all can arrange for them to visit us. We would definitely be very happy. We would like to write to them, but we don't have the address.

Hopefully we will receive a detailed letter from you soon, so we can see how the new generation looks. Ruthchen will nearly be half a lady soon, after all.

I have about 90 meters of 8mm film, on which everything about our life is recorded. As soon as I have the chance, I will send it to you all, and could you please send me back a copy. We have not watched it yet, because it would disturb us. It is a film about dead people.

And to close some business: the company Machold, of which I am the national trustee, is almost nearly working with prewar capacity in table furnishings, the so-called rayon sets. We already have a large contract with Brown & Kruger in New York, which is already being woven. Do you all have an interest in entering into a business relationship?

Also again thank you very much for your telegram and the intended financial help. For the New Year we wish you all the best and hope to see you soon, because if you do not come here soon, I intend to come to America for business in the next year.

All my loved ones, many heartfelt greetings and kisses, Paul.

My New School

I started a new school year in Bruntal, and I was enrolled in the class in accordance with my age. My father was a respected person in the community by then. He was a hero, a soldier who had fought the Nazis to bring us freedom. He was also a liberated victim of the Nazi occupation, and he was a successful director of a functioning nationalized textile factory.

The German population was replaced by all sorts of Czechoslovak citizens from all over the country. Most of them were people who were given the opportunity to start a new life. They were given houses confiscated from the Germans, so now they were homeowners themselves. Some of them were just running away from their previous life, in order to start a new life. Others were so-called gold diggers; they would take whatever they could lay their hands on, and vanish.

My teacher at the public school was a young man from south Moravia, from a town where there used to be a small but very well-known Jewish community of about 3,000. The Jews there were not liked too much by the other locals. Only about 100 of them survived the war. Most of the survivors were not too welcomed back. They found that their houses and other property had been given to the locals by the Nazis. The locals were not too enthusiastic about returning the property to its rightful owners. It was a strong motivation to the survivors to just keep on going.

My teacher surprised me one day with a lecture to the whole class about the economic role of Jews in the exploitation of the common Czech people. It was a tirade of hate, which Hitler would have been proud of. All the class was looking at me as if I was the guilty person who harmed those poor people in those Czech villages. As if I owned a local pub, and everyone owed money to me. As if I used my position and charged high interest on their debt, and as if I gradually enslaved them. Or, alternatively, as if I did the same as the owner of a local grocery store, and so on . . . Naturally, I did not feel too comfortable in the class at all. But I survived.

I felt even less comfortable when my parents arranged that I take private piano lessons, and my piano teacher became my school teacher's wife. This situation did not improve my dislike of the task to make use of the nice piano we had at home. So when my parents asked me what I would like to have for my next birthday, I chose to be granted an end to my piano lessons. This ensured that I do not play the piano now, and I am happy to use other more comfortable means to listen to music!

Another Concentration Camp.

As I said, we expected that this life in Bruntal would pick up where we left off before the war. However, things turned out very differently.

The Red Army left the country several months after our liberation, and Czechoslovakia was a democracy. However, the Communist Party got an upper hand in a postwar coalition government, and became the strongest party. And more importantly, Czechoslovakia was assigned to be a part of the area of Russian influence at a conference of Allies before the war ended in victory.

The status of almost a colony was finalized with the communist Putsch in February 1948. This time it was the Soviet Union who ruled. Czechoslovakian borders were now equipped with several rows of fences, strengthened with live electric power and with an army of guards ready to shoot. It was another concentration camp, somewhat better than Terezin, maybe, but it definitely lasted much, much longer.

~~~

Chapter Nine
Another Fight for Freedom

My First Job (1959)

I grew up in Communist Czechoslovakia, the Czechoslovak Socialist Republic (CSSR.) I finished my education at Technical University in Prague in 1959. I was enjoying my engineering studies at the University, and the Prague cultural life. There was a big difference in the standard of living in the capital city, and life in places outside the capital. And this difference increased with proximity to the border. When I graduated, I was given "the privilege" of an assigned mandatory location very close to the border, closer than anyone else in my class. It was hardly engineering work, at a State farm in a small town close to the southern border between Bohemia and West Germany. It was about 15 kilometers from the border, and the no-man's-land filled with barbed wire and armed guards seemed just like a concentration camp. When I complained to the allocation commission I was told, "We are pretty sure you are smart enough to get out of there very soon, considering your *talents.*" They obviously had a certain prejudice about the "smart talents" assumed to be natural to Jews.

I was officially still "permanently living" with my parents in northern Moravia, which was actually right across the whole country from the allocated mandatory work place at the State farm. This was until I became a holder of a wet one-room apartment located in a suburb south of Prague.

I wanted to return to Prague, and after a lot of effort I got a job with a uranium mining company in western Bohemia that had an office in Prague.

I found and rented a one room sleeping accommodation in a private family house in Prague. It was not too far from my official residence as listed in the Federation Office document. It was a one-room basement apartment, with a small bathroom attached. The apartment was a below ground half-basement with a small window close to the ceiling, and the walls were wet. However, it was my official place of residency in the capital city. Actually it still is.

It took an effort to get the apartment. First, I published a description of a new masonry drying method in several daily newspapers, and in a technical magazine. There was an extensive public response. The housing shortage in Prague was notorious at that time. But there were also a lot of old, wet basement apartments that were declared for health reasons not suitable for occupancy by the communist government. There were also owners of small private brick houses, many of which had wet walls on the bottom, and the owners could not afford to have this repaired by the standard methods. So I applied to the City of Prague for allocation of a wet basement apartment. It would be for developing and testing the masonry electro-osmosis drying method I had described in the newspapers. I wanted to prove the efficiency of the new drying method with a practical example. The city ordered its civil engineer to evaluate my proposal from a technical point of view. I explained the proposed idea to the engineer, and he agreed with my proposal, recommended its acceptance, and recommended allocation of a wet basement apartment for me.

Based upon this official allocation of a permanent residency in Prague, I was allowed to get work there independently of my current job with the mining company, with its headquarters located far away in western Bohemia. (The rule was a person could not be employed in Prague if his permanent residency was not in Prague. And one could not get permanent residency in Prague if he was not employed in Prague. It was a classic "Catch 22" situation.) So with this "new electro-osmosis drying method" development and testing plan, I by-passed the City of Prague "Catch 22" Rule.

After the "Prague Spring" Ended (1968)

Rose and I were married in 1965, and Hana, our elder daughter, was born in 1966. There was then a limited freedom of movement in the late 1960's, especially the "Prague Spring" of 1968. There were some tendencies to install a more democratic government, to lower the strictness of Russian rule, and to change at least somewhat the communist economic system towards a market economy. The Prague Spring movement stirred a hope for a free and better life. Practically, travel to the West became easier.

All that ended when the Russian Red Army, with armies of other neighboring communist countries, invaded Czechoslovakia on 21 August 1968. They had been welcomed in May 1945, but not at this time. However, for at least a while, there was still some residue of the Prague Spring freedom atmosphere in our Red

Army occupied country. Some travel to the West was still easier than it used to be under the standard communist rule.

My brother and I, with my family, left Czechoslovakia in 1968, and 1969, respectively. We were permitted to travel to the West for holidays for several weeks. We went to Munich in West Germany, and we stayed longer than permitted. Actually much longer, because we did not return at all.

We were refugees in West Germany, in Munich. I looked for a job, and responded to an advertisement about a structural engineer consultant looking for an assistant. I was hired, and did some structural design for him. He was very helpful and we had a friendly relationship. It turned out that he had been an SS officer stationed in Paris during the war. I did not even think about refusing to shake his hand. We parted on a very friendly basis when I had finished my work, although he told me he had hired me because he felt sorry for me. I swallowed this without any comment; I was a well-trained survivor already by that time.

After some adventures in Germany and Australia, we finally settled in the USA. Our parents visited us several times after they retired. As retired people they were permitted to travel, but we could not visit them in Czechoslovakia. We were sentenced, in our absence, to some prison terms, as we were told by our parents.

The End of an Era

My father passed away in 1985, when I was working for the US Army Engineers in South Korea. My mother survived three more years, and passed away in 1988. At that time she was ill, and could no longer travel. My mother and another Jewish lady were the only Jews in the town at the time my father passed away. The other Jewish lady had also survived Terezin and Auschwitz, and she settled in the same town as my parents did. She married and had two daughters, who were approximately the same age as my brother. The other Jewish lady became my mother's closest friend. She also had some other friends, and they all kept her company occasionally. My brother and I exchanged letters with her quite frequently, and we talked with her on the telephone often. Suddenly, she asked if our two daughters could visit her. They were planning to travel to Europe together, and so it seemed that this might be a good opportunity to see her once again.

Our younger daughter, Helen, had some friends in Europe from her days when we were in Korea and she attended the American High School in Seoul. This was the general arrangement there for the American and other Western children living in Seoul with their parents. My younger daughter received a visa from the Czechoslovakian consulate in Washington with no problems, as she had been born outside of Czechoslovakia, in Australia. And she was now a US citizen, as we all were. Our older daughter was in Europe at the time already. She was an exchange student studying in France. She applied for a visa at the Czechoslovakian consulate in Paris, and was told they would let her know whether or not a visa would be approved for her. She had been born in Czechoslovakia and, together with us, had stayed out of the country longer than permitted. Communist Czechoslovakia considered those who were born there to be Czechoslovak citizens for ever, if convenient. However, after a week or two she was contacted by the Czechoslovakian consulate in a very friendly manner. She was advised that she would be given the entry visa as she had wished.

The two sisters met in Paris and traveled around Western Europe. Finally, they arrived in Vienna. They were ready to cross the border. However, when I spoke with my mother on the telephone and told her that her granddaughters were ready to visit her, she asked angrily, "Whose silly idea was it to send them to Czechoslovakia now?" I opened my eyes and could answer this question to myself by myself: Had I forgotten how the communist state system would exploit to their advantage every tragic situation of their vulnerable citizens? I could see then how my ailing mother was being pressed by the communist authorities in Czechoslovakia to invite my daughters in. The authorities could then hold my daughters, and force me to come to Czechoslovakia as a condition of their release. I was still a wanted person there. The authorities knew that I was working for the US Army in South Korea, and they would not believe that I did not have any special information of interest to their North Korean friends. I could see all three of us being kept in communist Czechoslovakia for the rest of our days, probably imprisoned, and never see my mother, my wife, or each other again. So I called my daughters in Vienna and told them not to travel to Czechoslovakia at all; and in my mind I thanked my mother for giving me the message with such courage. She passed away several months later.

The communist system collapsed in Czechoslovakia in the fall of 1989, with the Velvet Revolution led by Vaclav Havel. It was a revolution without the loss of life. There was no vengeance for the past deeds of wrongdoing: no "vengeance is mine." Vaclav Havel, a humanitarian playwrite and anti-communist resistance leader, was elected the first President of the post-Cold War free Czechoslovakia.

I visited the country several years later. It was almost a quarter of a century since I had left with permission to leave for five weeks. I traveled around to the familiar places I used to know so closely. I visited my parents' burial place, and met with several old friends.

I also wanted to meet with the good Jewish lady who had taken care of my mother in her last days. We met in Prague. I wanted to thank her for the help she gave to my ailing mother, and we had a lot of things to talk about. She told me how she had suggested to my mother that mom could perhaps meet with me in Vienna, the capital of neighboring Austria, after the meeting with my daughters did not happen. My mother got furious and started screaming, and sent her away, which had upset the Jewish lady a lot. I could see the situation somewhat differently. Most people at that time knew about Austria being a communist agents' playground. Kidnapping of desired "emigrants" in Austria and dragging them across the border into Czechoslovakia was a common routine in those days. So my mother must have thought that her best friend was being used and forced by the communist police.

They resumed their friendship again after some time. It was in their mutual interest, after all. My mother needed her friendship and her help, and the good Jewish lady was to inherit my parents' nice furniture. In any event, their separation must have been a very sad time for them both.

One thing the good Jewish lady told me before we parted, and I will remember it forever: "There is a limit to everybody's heroism." Could this have been her own apology? Was she trying to clear her own conscience? After all, to strive for a morally clean conscience was heroism in itself; specifically in a country just liberated from being ruthlessly ruled by brutal empires for the last half century. Hopefully the children of the liberated generation will not have to clean their conscience too often. Hopefully the new children will have a happier life than the generation which experienced the oppression of those evil empires, and inherited the "bad dreams forever."

~~~

Appendices

A – Presentation to a High School in Redmond, WA

B – Certificate of Recognition

C – University of Washington Q&A

D – My Presentation Outline

E – Related Resources

Appendix A
Mission Accomplished
My Presentation at a High School in Redmond, WA

26 June 2011

I started my Holocaust presentation as usual:

I will tell you a story about a little innocent boy, who was locked up in prison for three years. He was actually sentenced to death, to be murdered, but his murderers were busy murdering others, so he survived. . . the little boy was actually me. . .

I have 90 minutes to tell my story of 9 years. . . then we make a break, a pit stop. . .

I finish with a note about the danger of hate: "and don't forget, don't hate each other; hate leads to war, we cannot afford another World War, it would eliminate the life on this planet, including yours, within seven and a half minutes, with the use of Cold War weapons. . . and those weapons are more advanced now.

We end in time for some questions and answers . . .

The students ask many questions:

"Who from your family survived, and who vanished among your family and friends?"

"Did you ever meet the children from the Heim again, or the supervisors?"

"How did you get out of Czechoslovakia?"

"How long have you been in the USA?"

And then they ask, "Why did you choose the USA?"

So I answer, "Well, the people in this country, the prevailing majority, are willing to fight for their freedom, that's why. . ."

A final standing ovation followed. . . and I knew that I was communicating with the young people now, that we understand each other and that they cherish the same values as I do; the same values as their parents do and as their teachers do. . .

The children's parents or their ancestors are from all over the world. Some of their ancestors came a long time ago from Africa, and some were in this country forever. Some came recently from India, from China, and from other places in Asia. Some parents came to work for Microsoft, others came to work for other companies, or they set up their own businesses. All of them cherish the freedom they enjoy in this country, and they will fight for it, putting up their own lives if necessary. . .

I wanted to join this party, too. . . and I did.

Appendix B
Certificate of Recognition from the Secretary of Defense

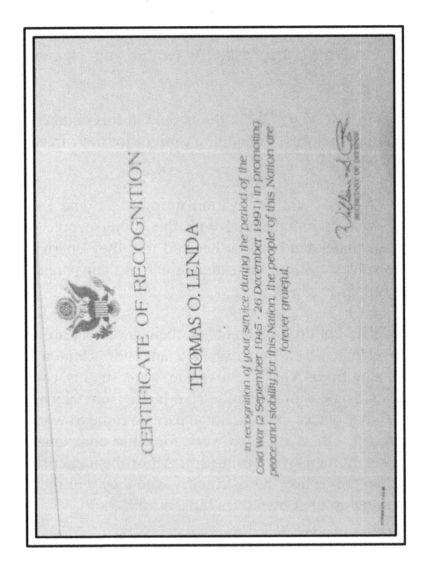

Appendix C
University of Washington Students
Questions and Answers

Note: this is a copy of questions asked by students of the University of Washington. Their questions were asked and transferred to me using the internet, prior to my presentation on 23 May 2012.Their class instructor read my biography to them, and the students had the opportunity to read this book on Kindle prior to the lecture. Then I answered the questions, and transferred my answers to the students prior to the lecture. This saved a lot of time, and added to the quality of my presentation, and the students' understanding.

The questions and answers have been edited here for better reading. Most of the answers were explained in the book and the presentation, but I include them here because the students' questions were interesting, and the answers shed additional light on the book.

"What was your relationship like with the other children in Terezin?"
"I missed the mandatory bullying because others were bigger targets. Mostly I was lonely. It did change over time. We knew we were all children on death row. We did not know what the Nazi plan was, but we saw the results: Our friends were disappearing, one after another."

"Did you go to school at Terezin? How did it operate? How was it kept hidden?"

"School was absolutely forbidden. But we managed to get warnings of SS inspections, and had time to hide everything."

"What languages were spoken in the camps?"

"In Terezin, mostly Czech and German."

"When you were nine years old, what was your understanding of what was happening?"

"There was unbelievable suffering in the overcrowded concentration camp. People were ill and hungry, and they would vanish into transports and never come back, including the children around me. . ."

"Did the adults explain everything?"

"Our supervisors did explain, as well as they could."

"Did your perception of events change over time, and if so, how?"

"Yes, more information became available over time. And rumors spread around."

"How were you reunited with your parents, and how did it feel?"

"My father picked us up. It was my 9th birthday."

"How was your family treated after the war?"

"We were heroes in the beginning, but then it had a tendancy to slip back into the usual routine. . . (The Jews are the Jews, you know. . .)"

"After World War II, what were the living conditions like for you?"

"Our family was living in a nice house, and I attended an ordinary school. There were still shortages of everything. There was rationing for five years after the war, and then there was never a situation of 'plenty' when the country was ruled by communists. To a certain extent, it was just another concentration camp."

"Why did your Uncle Otto flee to Shanghai?"

"Shanghai was the only place where there was not a visa requirement."

"Did he speak Chinese, or English?"

"He did not speak Chinese, but he did speak English."

"How do you feel about your fellow countrymen, particularly those who did not help those who were persecuted?"

"We were in touch with those who were kind to us. They took on a risk of persecution themselves for their kindness to Jews. We tried not to deal with the others, and they did not want to deal with us."

"Do you feel that justice was eventually done? If so, how?

"Most of the bad people were caught and sentenced, but not all of them. There was the well-publicized Nuremberg Process with the Nazi leaders. . . and later in Jerusalem with Eichmann, the Holocaust master."

"Has reconciliation taken place for you?
"Yes."

"Who were you angry with, and were you able to get over the pain?"
"I was not angry with all the Germans, but with most of them, then with less and less of them. I finally got over that, as the new generation could not be responsible for what had happened before they were born. I got over it, realizing that the German people were victims of an enforced bad propaganda. I saw Germany in rubble. I saw German beggars with only one leg. Germany lost 11.5 million military people in the war, and lots of civilians. They suffered for their belief in Hitler's perverse propaganda, and his promises to rule the world."

"How open have you been about these experiences throughout your life?"
"Mostly, I have preferred not to think or talk about it."

"What made you decide to share your stories?"
"I had some time to think about it after I retired. I felt that I owed something, as one who survived. . . I had Bad dreams. . ."

"How do you find the emotional courage to keep telling these stories?"
"It was and is with great difficulty."

"Have you gone through a difficult healing process?"
"Yes."

"Have you returned to any of the sites from your childhood?"
"Yes, I did. Some of the photos shown in the presentation were taken in 2005."

"Do people fully understand the Holocaust?"
"Hardly."

"If not, what are the misconceptions?"
"Let's close our eyes and forget it. . ."
"We will never be on the receiving side."

"What misconceptions lead to inaction over current genocide/mass killings?"
"Believing it can never happen to us. Silence and indifference to the suffering of others, or to the infringement of civil rights in any society can and will lead to genocide."

"How can we keep the Holocaust from happening again?"
"I do my best. . . Please, feel free to spread my message. Setting up and separating a group of people as the 'Bad Guys' to be murdered leads to war. With the

modern weapons available today, we cannot afford another war. Most likely the life on this planet would be finally terminated within thirty minutes."

"Is there a modern day movie which you feel best represents the conditions during the time of the Holocaust?"

"I don't think there is one specifically related to Terezin. There is the theater play, 'I Never Saw Another Butterfly," but it is hard to show and express those terrible happenings. The Nazis tried to make a propaganda movie, 'Hitler Gave a Town to the Jews.' It was a cause of additional mass murdering of a lot of people by reducing the population of the overcrowded Terezin concentration camp to make it a "Showplace Ghetto." There is a long list of videotapes available at the Washington Holocaust Education Center in Seattle."

"What is your stance on preserving versus allowing the camps to be taken over by nature?
"Preserving."

NOTE: "Transport from from Paradise," 1962. A Czech film directed by Zbyněk Brynych, is about Terezin.

NOTE: There is also a DVD by Tom and by James Carlson, based upon this book, titled 'Carrying the Ashes,' that is available. (See Appendix E)

Appendix D
Holocaust Survivor Presentation
by Thomas Lenda

Introduction

Hi, my name is Tom Lenda;

I want to tell a story about little Tommy, an innocent little boy, who was locked into a prison when he was six years old. The boy was kept in prison for three years. He was actually sentenced to death. He was supposed to be murdered, but his murderers were too busy murdering others. The murders ran out of time, and little Tommy survived. Just imagine, what kind of crime could a six year old boy have done to deserve three years of imprisonment and, finally, death? The little boy, that was me some 70 years ago. I have changed since then. Everybody changes with time. You will change as well.

I have divided my presentation into three parts:

Part I, 1936-1939, introduces our family and explains related historical circumstances.

Part II, 1939-1942, starts with the Nazi occupation of our country, until the time we were sent to prison, to Terezin Concentration Camp.

Part III, 1942-1945, deals with our life in Terezin Concentration Camp.

(NOTE: The book has a fourth part, the years after Terezin.)

Part I 1936-1939

A. Our Family

We lived in western Czechoslovakia before World War II.

I was born Tomas Lustig on 25 May 1936 in a town called Pilsen, in a country called Czechoslovakia, which is called the Czech Republic now.

We were a close-knit family: Lustigs, Spitz's, and Klaubers.

My father Pavel (Paul) Lustig (8/8/04-2/5/85)

Grandpa Bedrich Lustig, Uncles Fred & Otto Lustig

My mother Irene Spitz (8/2/09-1/8/88)

Grandma Olga Spitz, Uncles Leo & Pavu Spitz

We were well assimilated into the Czech community. We proudly considered ourselves to be Czechoslovakian citizens of Jewish origin (as they called us.)

B. Historical Circumstances

Czechoslovakia was politically a democratic island in central Europe at that time. The neighbor on the west was Nazi Germany, a very aggressive state. It was governed by Adolph Hitler, a brutal and reckless leader. He was full of hate. He was an aggressive public speaker, a master at activating his listeners' hate genes. Jews were persecuted in Nazi Germany very harshly.

Nazi Germany occupied Czechoslovakia in two phases: partly in 1938, and fully on 15 March 1939. In between those two times some Nazi sympathizers and agents blew up the Jewish cemetery in Pilsen, where we lived. However in doing so they also blew themselves up. Jews took courage from that, saying "God is on our side, and nothing can happen to us." It was not exactly what our family would say. Our motto was: "God helps those who help themselves."

Part II 1939-1942

A. Our Family After the Nazi Takeover

I was a three year old boy in 1939. My father escaped Pilsen the same day the Nazis invaded the country, and went to Prague, the capital city. My mother and I followed two weeks later. We settled in a rented house in Radesovice, a wooded area east of Prague.

The Nazis started to oppress local Jews in the same way as they did in Germany. New oppressive regulations were issued frequently. For example: employment restrictions, sale of property restrictions, education restrictions, shopping restrictions, use of transportation restrictions, movement restrictions, and others. Then starting 1 September 1941 all Jews had to wear a yellow star on their clothes, with the word "*Jude*" (Jew in German.)

Our family would be deported to Terezin Concentration Camp on 12 September 1942. My Uncle Frank escaped to Slovakia and joined the anti-Nazi underground resistance. My Uncle Otto escaped to

Shanghai, China. My Grandpa Bedrich Lustig, my Uncles Leo and Pavu (Paul) Spitz, and Grandma Olga Spitz, were sent to Terezin. They went earlier than we did, and were sent from Terezin to extermination camps in parts of eastern Europe occupied by the Nazis. They were all murdered there.

B. Oppressive Regulations in Practice

In Radesovice, my father was allowed to do manual labor only. He had been a business representative of a textile factory. I was not allowed to go to school. Nazi Germany started a war, and there were shortages of everything, especially food. Rationing of food was imposed. Meat was especially hard to get. The Black Market became common, though illegal.

This is what happened to our Jewish neighbor Wilma, and my Uncle Pavu. They road bikes to buy some meat from farmers in a nearby village one evening. A policeman stopped them on their way back. He took them to a police station for questioning. The result was they were sent to Terezin concentration camp on the next available transport. We never saw Wilma and her daughter again. They were gone when we got to Terezin, murdered in one of the death camps in the East. My Uncle Pavu was still in Terezin when we arrived, but he was sent on a transport later and did not return.

There was another Jewish family next door: The Riesels. They had two boys of my age, Peter and John. I played with them. They were gone one day on a transport to Terezin, and we never saw them again. They perished also.

Part III 1942-1945

A. Our Trip to Terezin

Our family was transported to Terezin from Bubny station in Prague in September of 1942. We traveled by train from Radesovice into the city center of Prague. We were allowed to take 50 kilograms (about 110 pounds) of personal belongings per person with us. The assembly place was in the Prague Exhibition Hall, where we joined about 1,000 other Jews, mostly from Prague. We went by an ordinary passenger train, 2nd and 3rd class, except we had to walk the last three miles from Bohusovice to Terezine. I myself had a small backpack, which was full of batteries and two flashlights. I was very proud of it because, even though only six years old, I was also helping.

Terezin was a small military base, about 200 years old. It had been built for about 6,000 military people, but there were 58,491 prisoners there when we arrived, as I now know. The day of our arrival, 156 prisoners died. In total, there were 139,654 Jewish prisoners sent to Terezin during the Nazi occupation. Of these, about 33,430 (24%) were killed there.

We were taken to a check-in hall, something like a customs hall. It was called *Slojska*. *"Slojsovat"* meant "to steal" in the local slang. Nazi officers checked each bag, and took whatever they liked.

B. The First Day

Our new home was in a huge, dark attic, on top of a three story barracks building. We shared it with a lot of other people, as well as mice and rats. The beds were straw-filled sacks on plywood sheets laid across large beams on the floor. There were many sick people lying there; some would die during the night. I saw the dead people being carried out on stretchers in the morning.

There was no privacy except the darkness. But we did have our batteries and flashlights. Toilets and washrooms used in common. They were one level down which, as you can imagine, was somewhat awkward for a six year old boy. But I made it without accidents – most of the time.

The food was served military style, on metal trays. I did not like the food, but I ate it. Hunger was the best cook. We learned that the main features of life in this concentration camp were:

Constant feeling of an empty stomach,

Fleas and bed bugs,

Close presence of death and, especially,

Permanent threat to be sent in a transport to the East.

We thought that nothing could be worse, but we braved it out. What else could we do?

C. Getting a Work Assignment

The only way to get out of the dark attic was to get a work assignment. My mother was a certified (registered) nurse, a profession very much appreciated in Terezin. There was a large hospital in one of the barracks, and sleeping quarters for the nurses came with it. It was a crowded place. There were bunk beds in the nurses' quarters stacked three levels high. My father found a job in the Transportation Corps. We used to live as a family in a nice, comfortable apartment. Now we all had to live separately in barracks.

D. My New Home

What to do with me, a six year old boy? Terezin had homes for children of all ages, called a "Home," or *"Heim"* in German. It was like a boarding school, but without the school. Nazis forbade the teaching of Jewish children. My mother took me to the Heim I was allocated to. I was totally confused. I was scared she would leave me there and walk away, and she did.

My Heim was a large, one-room establishment, in another old barracks building, on the second floor. Bunk beds were the main furniture. There was a large table under two windows on the other side of the room from the door. There were a lot of boys there. Gerta was our supervisor. She gave me an introductory speech about daily routines and rules. She also warned me I should expect to receive a lot of bullying. (I was a newcomer, so that was almost mandatory.) Luckily for me, the boys already had another victim at that time.

E. Life in the Heim

I remember four supervisors: Gerta, Hanka, Erna, and a German lady. They were teachers by profession, but we were not allowed to call them teachers. Gerta got married, against the rules, and the newlyweds were immediately sent in a transport to the East. We did not hear of them again. Hanka then became the main supervisor, and we got Erna as an assistant.

I was very lonely, although there were lots of children around me and my parents visited me as often as they could. My mom would sometimes come in the evening and bring some extra food for me. Then she would go and visit my adopted brother, Rudi, on the same mission. This extra food for me was not popular with my peers and the supervisors. My mom had to bring it when everyone was supposed to be sleeping, but nobody was. The extra food did not help in my loneliness. I wanted to become a qualified member of the gang. I wanted to belong. But, I was hungry, too. I lost the brand of being a newcomer very slowly, but I learned the needed routines as time passed by, and I felt much better after some time. We all held together, and covered up for each other. My life as a prisoner became less sad and more bearable as time went by.

F. The Orphans

I started to realize that I was actually one of the few lucky ones. Most of the children did not have parents around, as I had. Their parents had already been sent by the so-called "working transports" to the East, and had to leave their children behind.

Some parents made arrangements with relatives or volunteers to "adopt" their children. The children were already orphans, and they felt it inside. The only real substitute for the missing parental love was their close friendship with each other. The percentage of orphans grew with time. Then the orphans themselves started to vanish into transports to "join" their parents. Practically speaking, the orphans were already on a death roll. Actually, we all were, but the orphans were at the head of the line.

Our "crime" was that we were born as Jews. According to the Nazis, the world had to be rid of us. We did not know exactly what the Nazi plan was, we just saw the results: our friends were gone, one friend after another. New children arrived, and some would go soon after their arrival. It was a race against time. It was a question of whether the Nazi murdering machine would collapse before our turn to be murdered would come. In the end, only a very few of us survived.

G. Our Terezin Adventures

Terezin was a very crowded place, with many people everywhere. Children were not supposed to be in the streets without supervision, but sometimes we managed to sneak out of the Heim.

Most of the housing was in old blocks of apartment houses, with separated courtyards. The prisoners made holes in the separating walls, and connected the yards, and the locations of those openings created a maze. This was our secret knowledge: we used those connections to move around the town without using the streets. When we had to cross a street, we would do it fast, and disappear into the next block. And so we would go places where we were not supposed to be. We loved electrical maintenance shops; every one of us wanted to be an electrician. Occasionally someone would point out to us we were not supposed to be there. But we were getting street smart, by Terezin standards.

H. Train Rides

We loved to watch the construction of the new railway spur coming into Terezin from Bohusovice. Later, we would climb on the cattle trains being shifted from one siding to another, to catch a ride. It had an element of danger for us. Then one day an SS officer appeared from out of nowhere. The SS officers were the most fanatic and brutal of the Nazi murdering machine. The officer jumped on a platform behind one little boy and hit him so hard that the boy fell to the ground from the moving train. He lay there for a while, before some Terezin prisoners showed up and carried him away. The story of this spread around the children's Heims quickly, and it was the end of our free rides on the moving cattle trains. Actually, most of the "free rides" were reserved for the prisoners allocated to a one way trip: The Transport to the East.

Our Heim moved several times, mostly for the better. We moved into the former Post Office building on a corner of the main square. Across was the SS management building, called the Commadature. We watched the SS through our windows as they were marching, or traveling in their automobiles to their work place. The Nazis had a high privacy fence built around the streets they used, so they would not have to mix with the Jews. There were little gates made in the fence for the Jews to cross the street when there were no Nazis in sight.

I. Forbidden School

The Jews made an extreme effort to educate their children, and it was the most effective resistance in Terezin. This teaching was forbidden by the Nazis; Jews took a dangerous risk to teach their children. The punishment was simple. Violators would be on the next transport to the East. They would be at the head of the roll for death.

There were no official schools in Terezin, so our "school" was the Heim were we lived. Jews smuggled all sorts of educational materials into the concentration camp. We would finish our chores in the morning, then set up a blackboard and sit around our meal table.

Hanka would teach us the alphabet, and to read and write and count.

Hanka would tell us stories from history and natural science.

Hanka would read to us in the evening, if we behaved.

Sometimes a Rabbi would come to teach us.

Sometimes an accordion player would come and play popular songs.

I was able to enroll in a regular school class according to my age after the war, a result of the secret teaching effort in Terezin.

J. SS Inspection: A Close Call

Once an SS officer came to inspect our Heim. Rumor had it that a boy had been seen walking, wearing a typical school backpack. A policeman asked him where he was going. The boy said "to school," and this was reported to the Nazi management. The SS started to plan an inspection, but the Jewish Elders found out about it and sent a warning to all the Heims. We quickly removed and hid anything that could imply teaching. The inspection ended as a success for the Jews: no special allocations to the next transport were made because of this incident.

K. Culture

Another resistance was the cultural performances of artists. It lifted the spirits of the prisoners, but most of the performers were sent to the extermination camps as soon as the Nazis noticed their activity.

L. Children's Work Assignment

Children my age were given a special work assignment. We would be taken outside the camp limits to the busy crematorium and columbarium. There we would load onto carts the cardboard boxes bearing the ashes of deceased prisoners. These boxes would then be dumped into the Ohře River outside the walls. Of the 139,656 prisoners who came to Terezin, about one quarter, or 33,430, died there because of the harsh living conditions.

M. Soccer

Soccer was the sport in Terezin. There was even a league competition followed enthusiastically by many prisoners. There was no regular soccer field in Terezin, so games were played in the barracks courtyards.

We kids would also play soccer, for exercise and fun, using small, handmade balls filled with old rugs. I was not too good, so my parents arranged with my Uncle Frank to train me. Frank was a local soccer star. It did not improve my performance too much, but it improved my image as a soccer player among my peers, at least for a while.

N. Children's Hospital

I was sent to the children's hospital frequently when I was sick. Two of my mom's aunts came to visit me one day, and brought a little piece of yellow pound cake they must have saved from their own small rations. They asked me if I would eat the pound cake, knowing I was a very picky eater. I responded, "I will eat anything," and it made them cry. That was their goodbye visit. They vanished into a transport soon after, and we never saw them again.

O. Red Cross Visit and Propaganda Film

The Nazis began a great cover-up project to prepare for a planned Red Cross visit in June of 1944. And there was also a film-making activity in progress. We were given new white shirts for attending the performance and we could keep them. It was supposed to be a propaganda film called "Hitler Gave a Town to the Jews."

P. Little Girl on Death Row

I still remember my last stay in the children's hospital. It was during a period of high transport activity, in the fall of 1944. Next to me in bed was a sick girl, one of those who had been selected for the next transport to the East. She and her mother were supposed to leave the next morning. She was one year older than me, so she was probably 9 at the time. I was not a very tactful child. I asked her how it feels, to be selected to die. She was not shocked by my question, as it was actually quite a real possibility. (We still did not know exactly what happened in the East, but we knew it was a place of no return.) Her answer was, "What will be will be," and this shocked me. That was not an expression used in our family at all.

I asked her if she would do something about it, and she answered there was nothing to be done. I suggested she disappear into the streets and hide somewhere until the transport was gone. Her answer was that someone else would just have to go instead of her. She said there might be a possibility she and her mother would meet up with her father there. He had gone in a "working transport" to the East earlier. She was gone in the morning when I woke up, and I never saw her again.

We were suspicious about the statement that children were going to join their parents in those "East places." This was the destination of the transports as we knew it. We did not know of names like "Auschwitz." We did not know about the gas chambers either. Going to the "East" just meant going to a place of no return.

Q. My Father Leaves

The allocation to the transport to the east caught up with my father in the fall of 1944. We were very sad, for we did not know if we would ever see him again. All we could do was to hope for the best.

I qualified as a half-orphan within our gang as soon as my father left. So I grew in the ranks of the gang, but it was poor compensation for a missing father.

Only a memory was left with us: how his spirit was always high, expecting the end of the war at any time soon, how he would talk about every cultural performance in Terezin, how the performers kept vanishing in the transports, how he took me to the Brundibar children's opera performance in the attic of one of the barracks.

R. The Spring of 1945

We had been imprisoned in Terezin for two and a half years, however, there was something new for us to see almost every day towards the end of the war. We saw small airplanes flying high up in the sky. We saw a red glow in the northern sky for several nights. Rumor had it that it was the burning city of Dresden. The Nazis had been developing chemical and biological weapons there.

S. Death March

One event I will never forget is a death march that came to Terezin. We went one day to the main incoming street where the Nazi/Jewish separation fence used to be. Now the fence was gone, and there was a wall of onlookers. We saw a group of probably not more than fifty very thin and dirty people, and they were just drifting along the street. A dirty blue and white striped uniform was hanging on each of them. There was a cordon of Terezin prisoners holding hands and walking alongside the drifting people, to separate them from the onlookers. Some of the drifters were falling as they went. They were picked up by other Terezin prisoners, placed on stretchers, and carried away.

Suddenly one of the onlookers threw several little pieces of yellow pound cake into the middle of those drifting people. Those who were close to it grabbed the pieces of cake from the street, and those who did not get a piece tried to take it away from the lucky ones. It was like a chicken fight at feeding time.

Most of the people just kept drifting along, with the apathy of drifters. They had forgotten any sense of human dignity a long time before. They just kept doing what they had been doing a while ago. Survival instinct was all they had. The drifters were survivors of the "working transports" to the East. They were placed into isolated housing because they were sick, mostly with typhus.

T. The End of the War

The typhus spread around anyway, and Terezin was placed under quarantine. The concentration camp was isolated from the rest of the outside world when the war ended. Nobody was supposed to leave Terezin. It was probably at that time my mother made a promise to God: she would stay in the hospital where she worked as long as needed and take care of the patients, if my father would return to us safely.

My father had been sent to Auschwitz concentration camp in the fall of 1944. He escaped from a death march with a little group of prisoners as the Red Army approached. He then joined a Czechoslovakian Army unit in order to fight the Nazis, not knowing that his brother Fred was already with them

My father met my Uncle Fred and they were reunited a little later. My father learned that Fred had routinely changed his name, to provide cover when he was with the Slovak underground resistance. Uncle Fred's last name was Lenda at the time, and my father accepted the same name, changing it from Lustig.

Uncle Fred asked my father if there was anything he could get for him. My father told him he had all he needed now. However, he would like a violin, because he missed his music. A not so new but nice violin arrived several days later.

My father and uncle took part in the final liberation fights, and they both received medals for their bravery and efforts.

My father came back to Terezin to retrieve his family. It was on 25 May 1945, my ninth birthday. We traveled to Prague together. Then my mother returned to Terezin to fulfill her promise to God to continue her duties as a nurse in the hospital, helping the victims of the typhoid epidemic. I traveled with my father to his army unit and started to attend a regular school. Our family was united again one month later, after Terezin was finally emptied, and closed.

Summary

I told you about:
1. The time from 1936 to 1939
This was about our family, where we lived, and about the historical circumstances.
2. The time from 1939 to 1942
This was about the time from the start of the Nazi occupation of our country until the time we were sent to Terezin.
3. The time from 1942 to 1945
This was about our life in the prison, the concentration camp, until the end of the war, and our liberation.

(In addition, in this book I have told you about the experiences of my father and uncle, and many of the events after the end of the war.)

Conclusion

A. Czech Jews Fate – The Extinct Race

The Nazi plan was to cleanse Europe of the Jews. They even started a "Museum of an Extinct Race." They stored confiscated Jewish religious items in several warehouses in Prague during the war. The museum survived, and is now called The Jewish Museum in Prague. But there are practically no live Jews left in the Czech Republic. There were 118,310 Jews there before the war, in 1939. There were about 3,700 Jews in the Czech Republic in 2006. As far as the territory of the Czech Republic is concerned, the Nazis very nearly succeeded in their cleansing effort.

B. The fate of the Children

There were 18,033 children in the territory of the current Czech Republic at the beginning of the war. Some 15,000 went to Terezin. Almost all of those vanished in the transports to the east, such as Auschwitz, to be murdered upon arrival. Only 700 of us were left in Terezin at the end of the war. In my age group of 9 years and younger, there were only 48 of us left.

There is one thing we should agree on with the Nazis: "The children are the most precious asset a nation has." By concentrating on murdering the children, the Nazi plan kept working years after the Nazis were gone.

You know, there are still children targeted for extinction even today.

I was one of them.

I hope that you will be one of those who will help to bring an end to all genocide, no matter where in the world it might be.

Thanks for listening.

Appendix E
Other Works Based Upon This Book

"Pavel's Violin: A Song of Hope"

 This is an historical novel by Walter William Melnyk, about the "not so new but nice violin," and the life of Pavel (Paul) Lustig. Available from Amazon, Barnes & Noble, and most other online booksellers. ISBN: 978-1539335221.

"Pavel's Violin is a work of historical fiction, a genre that, at its best, serves as a metaphor that can draw a reader into a story as a first hand participant, rather than as a consumer of facts. This is what I have tried to do with the story of "Pavel's Violin." I hope you will not just learn about what happened, but that you will become part of the story, yourself. That you will stand beside Jakob atop Kartellerjochl, with Pavel in a cattle car transport on its way to Auschwitz, with Nurse Ilse and her children as Zyklon B pellets fall among them in the gas chamber. And more. I hope you will not only hear the Violin, but will experience the playing of it. The sound of its music under your left ear. The vibrations of the wood upon your chin and shoulder. Most of all, I hope you, too, will realize the compulsion of the story, and the obligation to recount it, in your own way, to others.

"I had not set out to tell the story of Pavel and his Violin. Even as I began to gather information, even as I wrote the opening chapters, I was certain that I would never complete the project. I did not believe I had the right, or the ability, to tell this tale. But as I learned more and more of the story, as I actually played the Violin that Pavel had played, I began to believe I had an obligation to try. When that sense of obligation became a sense of compulsion, I finally gave in; so much so that I became a Jew myself, through adoption into Humanistic Judaism. I still question whether I have the ability to tell the tale as it deserves to be told. But who will tell it, in the years to come, if our humility should always be an excuse to avoid our obligation/"

This story is inspired by the memoir of Tommy Lustig, Pavel's son, *Children on Death Row*, also available on Amazon.

All author royalties from the sale of *Pavel's Violin* are donated to the United States Holocaust Museum, and other Holocaust Memorials."

For more information, visit
www.pavelsviolin.com

~ Walter William Melnyk

"Carrying the Remains: A Boy's Promise to the Children of Terezin"

This is a musical drama video produced by Dr. James Carlson, a composer and former Professor of Music at the University of the South in Sewanee, Tennessee, where *Carrying the Remains* was produced and first performed. Dr. Carlson is married to the Czech violinist, Lucie Carlson, who is a relative of Tommy Lustig. The Carlsons, with their two children, have recently returned to Lucie's home in Prague. They are famous for their performances as "Cricket and Snail," a violin and accordion duo.

"This work combines a concert work with music, theater, dance and visual media to tell the poignant story of Jewish Holocaust survivor Tom Lenda (Tommy Lustig.) It's called *Carrying the Remains: A Boy's Promise to the Children of Terezin.*

The premier of *Carrying the Remains* took take place on April 2, 2015, and featureed both the University's Music and Theater Departments. Dr. Carlson has composed the music and edited the script, David Landon, Professor of Theatre Arts and Speech, narrates, Courtney World, Visiting Assistant Professor of Theatre Arts and Speech set the choreography, and César Leal, Sewanee Symphony

Orchestra Conductor and Assistant Professor of Music conducts the chamber orchestra. Together with a number of University students a significant work has been created that fluidly combines narration, music, dance and projected imagery. The result is something rarely seen, and profoundly moving.

"The idea for the project started soon after I had married my wife Lucie who is from the Czech Republic. I'm from Seattle and on Lucie's first visit to my family she mentioned she had a relative, a cousin of her mom, in the Seattle area with whom her family had lost contact. After a little research we found that he lived just a half an hour away from where I grew up!

"So we soon met Tom Lenda and his wife Rose. We learned of his childhood experience as a prisoner in the Terezin concentration camp in the Czech Republic. Tom had written a book about his story and had been giving Holocaust presentations in the schools for several years.

"On one of our visits, Tom mentioned to me that he would like to preserve his story in some sort of musical or theatrical form. I told him I would think about it and look for opportunities. After a while, I saw the resources line up at the University of the South where I teach to create a chamber orchestra work with narrator and dancers. I thus started talking to my colleagues and began work on the piece while I was in the Czech Republic last summer (2014.) I even visited Terezin during this time to further deepen my understanding of Tom's experiences.

"It has been a powerful journey working on this project. I found it especially striking the way in which Tom's story starkly juxtaposes the traumatic with the childishly playful. To a large extent, I had to embody Tom's experiences to create the music and edit the piece's text and this was often emotionally very difficult. Throughout the process, however, I was always reassured by the importance of the mission of telling and preserving Tom's story and raising Holocaust awareness.

"The premier of Carrying the Remains will take place on April 2, 2015, and will feature both the university's Music and Theater Departments. I have composed the music and edited the script, David Landon will narrate, Courtney World will set the choreography and César Leal will conduct the chamber orchestra. I am very pleased to have such great collaborators. Together with a number of our students we are creating a significant work that will fluidly combine narration, music, dance and projected imagery. The result promises to be something rarely seen and profoundly moving.

"We are also fortunate to have David Meola, a Jewish studies scholar who is currently teaching in the History Department, to bring a greater historical context to the performance of Carrying the Remains. He has planned a conference on genocides before the performance called "Sewanee Remembers."

(more info: **http://yomhashoah.sewanee.edu**)

This event will be further enriched by visits by Tom Lenda and Holocaust scholar Dagmar Herzog who will both give presentations and interact with students and the Sewanee community.

"So here's what we're planning to make sure Carrying the Remains with its unique synthesis of the arts and humanities gets documented and shared. In this kick-starter campaign, our goal is to raise $4000. This would enable us to do the following: The 50-minute performance and dress rehearsals will be filmed using a 3 or 4 camera set up. The resulting footage will be edited to effectively present the multifaceted nature of this piece. 1000 copies of the resulting DVD would then be produced. Interviews, talks and panel discussions of the "Sewanee Remembers" conference may also be included on the DVD.

"Copies of the DVDs will then be sent to various schools and Holocaust and Jewish Studies libraries free of charge to be part of their collections. The remaining copies will be available for sale online and at subsequent performances of Carrying the Remains with the proceeds going to the Tennessee Holocaust Commission.

http://www.tennesseeholocaustcommission.org/"

The DVD is now available for viewing on YouTube at

https://youtu.be/XcEyGMuMe_M

For more information about Cricket and Snail, Visit

http://www.alembickmusic.com/cricketandsnail.html

~ James Carlson.

Made in the USA
Coppell, TX
26 December 2019